GOLF
SCHOOL

GOLF SCHOOL

JOHN LEDESMA

PRC

First published in 1999 by
PRC Publishing Ltd,
Kiln House, 210 New Kings Road, London SW6 4NZ

This edition published 2000
Distributed in the U.S. and Canada by:
Sterling Publishing Co., Inc.
387 Park Avenue South
New York, NY 10016

© 1999 PRC Publishing Ltd

ISBN 1-85585-868-1
Printed and bound in China

CONTENTS

PART 2:
RULES & EQUIPMENT

PART 3: GOLF SCHOOL

HISTORY

The publisher wishes to thank Allsport for supplying the photographs on the following pages:
This spread, 23 (*bottom*), 29 (*left*), 32 (*bottom*), 35, 36, 41, 42-43, 46, 50-51 (*both*), courtesy of Allsport/David Cannon
11 courtesy of Allsport/Simon Bruty
12, 27 (*top*), courtesy of Allsport/Hulton Deutsch
17, 27 (*bottom*), 28, 32 (*top*), 48, courtesy of Allsport/Stephen Munday
22 courtesy of Allsport

HISTORY

Golf historians claim to know a great deal about the origins of golf. Exactly how far back the great stick-and-ball games go will never be known. Maybe some day an archeologist will unearth the remains of a Pleistocene cave dweller clutching a tree branch with grooves on the face. Many civilizations and cultures take credit for the game's origins, and debate has raged for many centuries. It doesn't matter: the important thing is, golf thrives today and still can't be mastered.

PREDECESSORS

Of course, Scotland has the most solid claim as the home of golf. But other societies have indulged in activities that resemble what today is called golf. In the third century BC the Romans played a game called *pangea* or *paganica*. Many historians prefer to regard pangea as an early form of hockey; at all events, it involved propelling a feather-filled ball with a bent stick.

The Chinese get in on the action with their game *ch'ui wan* which was first played around AD 950. Players attempted to advance their ball into a series of pits. Lies were tough back then. In Britain, *cambuca* was a popular pastime in which a wooden ball was knocked about at several targets. In Belgium they still play a game called *chole*. This, however, is played by two teams that attempt to strike a beech-wood ball toward a target across a field. The game spread to northern France, where it is called *soule*.

A few cross-country versions of stick and ball were popular around the 17th century. *Jeu-de-mail* has origins in Italy and France and in its first forms was played over some distance, the goal being to hit a far-away door or tree in fewer whacks than your opponent. The English took it up as *palle-maille* (ball-mallet) and adapted it to be played in city streets or on purpose-built courts. Pall Mall, a famous street in the West End of London, is believed to have been built on or near the site of the first of these courts, close to St. James's Palace. *Kolven* is a Dutch game that old paintings often show taking place on a frozen lake or river. Players would attempt to strike their balls against a post or some other marker in fewer strokes than their opponents.

It is evident that there are many possible antecedents of what evolved into the modern game of golf. This is true of nearly every ancient game. There is little debate, though, that golf was formalized on the wind swept coastland of Scotland.

REVOKING THE RITE

In mid-15th century, an Act of Parliament in Scotland banned the playing of "Fute-ball, Golfe and uther sik unproffitabill sportis" for fear that they were luring men away from compulsory archery practice. (They were, after all, at odds with the English at this time.) This decree is the earliest known written mention of the sport. Of course, many golfers in Scotland must have been spending quite a bit of time on the links to warrant outlawing the game. Several more bans were attempted, but the country's fascination with golf would not be dampened. Archery and other forms of combat practice would have to wait.

Royal attitudes changed as early as the turn of the century, however, thanks to James IV of Scotland, who fell in love with the game. It is believed that James (of the family Stuart) commissioned a set of golf clubs from an artisan accustomed to fashioning bows and arrows for the soldiers. James obviously recognized the advantages of custom-made clubs: he later had a second set made especially for a match with the Earl of Bothwell. The Scottish royals supported golf for nearly two centuries following, the most enthusiastic golfing Stuart being Mary, Queen of Scots (whose third husband was grandson of the golf-playing earl).

In 1603 Mary's son, James VI, took the throne of England as James I and continued the royal promotion of the sport, although he insisted that no golf was to be played on Sundays until after church. It was during this time that he built a seven-hole course at Blackheath, then a small village a few miles east of London. (Royal Blackheath, founded in 1766, stands today as England's oldest golf club.) The first international golf match is believed to have involved the Scottish James II and a commoner partner against two English royals.

THE COMMITTEE

Throughout the 17th century and into the middle of the 18th, golf was popular but largely unorganized. The sport survived and thrived on wager and will. It was in 1744 that the Honourable Company of Edinburgh Golfers came into being in Edinburgh, Scotland. With an eye toward creating an undisputed golf champion, the company put together the first set of rules, known as the Thirteen Articles. A few of the more quaintly phrased appear below:

Rule 5 If your ball comes among water, or any watery filth, you are at liberty to take out your ball and bringing it behind the hazard and teeing it, you may play it with any club and allow your Adversary a stroke for so getting out your ball.

Rule 10 If a ball be stopp'd by any person, horse or dog, or anything else, the ball so stopp'd must be played where it lyes.

Rule 13 Neither trench, ditch or dyke made for the preservation of the links, nor the Scholar's Holes or the soldier's lines shall be accounted a hazard but the ball is to be taken out, teed and play'd with any iron club. (This was a purely local rule to cover conditions peculiar to Leith links, then just outside the city of Edinburgh.)

These were the rules that governed match play. John Rattray won the inaugural competition and was awarded a Silver Club.

ST. ANDREWS

Ten years after Edinburgh held its championship, the Society of St. Andrews Golfers was launched with a competition, the prize for which was a silver club. At that time golf was generally played on common (that is, public) land, and the number of holes varied considerably, depending on the space available. Until the 1750s it had been the custom at St. Andrews to play a round of 22 holes; but later a round there was fixed at 18 holes, and such was the prestige and influence of the St. Andrews club that this became the universally accepted number of holes for a round. The society eventually became the Royal & Ancient Golf Club of St. Andrews, and today it is known colloquially throughout the golfing world as the "R&A."

The Honourable Company was obliged to move to Musselburgh, on the south of the Firth of Forth east of Edinburgh, because the links land at Leith had been encroached upon by expansion of the city. Henceforward, St. Andrews came to be regarded as the home of golf and its world authority.

EXPANSION

As the Scots scattered about the globe, so did golf. There are records of shipping orders out of Leith that call for several clubs and several hundred balls to be shipped to Charleston, South Carolina, in 1743. This suggests there was play on the Carolina coast long before it became the major golf destination it is today. There is also evidence of golf played in Savannah, Georgia, a little later. Both clubs are thought to have perished by or during the Revolutionary War.

British expatriates and soldiers formed golf clubs all over the world. Wealthy Brits who regularly wintered in south-west France founded mainland Europe's first club at Pau in 1856. Scots names featured largely in the list of members, as they also did in the founders of the Calcutta Club in 1829 (later to become Royal Calcutta) and Bombay in 1842. As the Empire took root in Asia, clubs were established in places like Hong Kong, Taiping (Malaysia) and Bangkok (Thailand). The first Japanese course was constructed only in 1901 near Kobe. The Southern Hemisphere was discovering golf about the same time, with the creation of Royal Adelaide in Australia in 1870 and South Africa's Royal Cape Club in 1885. The first

recognized golf club in North America was the Royal Montreal Golf Club, which originated in 1873 and still operates today.

The 1890s witnessed a tremendous spurt in the construction of golf courses in Britain and in the United States as increasingly more expatriates crossed over and more Americans caught on. In 1888, the St. Andrew's Golf Course opened in Yonkers, New York. While golfers had been playing in various fields—such as John Reid's cow pasture—St. Andrew's is recognized as the first American golf club. (It was Reid and his "Apple Tree Gang" cronies who founded the club.) Herbert Warren Wind, perhaps the most distinguished American writer on golf, has suggested there were fewer than 12 golfers in the United States at that time. Six years later there were more than 80 courses, including historic sites such as Shinnecock Hills Golf Club on Long Island in New York, Newport Golf Club in Rhode Island, The Country Club at Brookline in Boston, Massachusetts, and the Chicago Golf Club in Illinois. As the millennium dawned, there were almost 1,000 clubs in America, which is more than there were in Britain.

On both sides of the Atlantic and elsewhere, golf was mainly a private affair reserved for the wealthy and the social elite. But in 1896–97 American commoners were given a break

with the opening of Van Cortland Park in New York City—the nation's first public course. By 1927, there were 4,000 U.S. golf courses. There were 1,500 in Britain at that time.

THE NATIONAL CHAMPIONSHIPS

In the British Isles, competition between the older clubs and between individual players intensified in the middle decades of the 19th century. The best player of the day was the Scot Allan Robertson (1815–58), who was the first man to break 80 at St. Andrews. Robertson, whose assistant was Old Tom Morris, was also the preeminent producer of feathery golfballs. What became the first British Open was held at Prestwick, on the Ayrshire coast, in October 1860 and was won by Willie Park of Musselburgh. That Open was the first true stroke-play championship ever held. In 1885 at Hoylake, near Liverpool, the British Amateur Championship was held for the first time, and was won by Allan Macfie—a feat not officially recognized until the event was taken over by the R&A 35 years later. The first U.S. Amateur Championship was conducted in 1895 at Newport. The winner was Charles Blair Macdonald, of the Chicago Golf Club. In a completely anti-climactic tournament by today's standards, Horace Rawlins won $150 in the first-ever U.S. Open, which was held at Newport the next day, and for which there were less than a dozen participants. These four events would become golf's early majors.

MOVERS AND SHAKERS

Macdonald, whose family came from Scotland, was as important to the development of the game in the United States as John Reid. Macdonald traveled overseas to school at the University of St. Andrews in Scotland, where he was introduced to golf by his grandfather. He is rumored to have bought his first set of clubs from Old Tom Morris and played against many of the best British golfers of the day. Upon his return to America, there was little opportunity to participate in the game. He solved this dilemma by designing the Chicago Golf Club and went on to design the National Golf Links of America, not far from Shinnecock Hills at Peconic Bay, Long Island, drawing much inspiration from his beloved Scottish courses.

Macdonald entered but failed to win either the U.S. Amateur or the U.S. Open in 1894, and was not happy about how it all played out. (These two inaugural occasions are not recognized today.) He told everyone who would listen that there needed to be a governing body for golf in America.

Macdonald's protests, among other things, resulted in the formation that year of the Amateur Golf Association of the United States (AGA), which eventually became the United States Golf Association (USGA). Macdonald held court at the inaugural gathering of the AGA, which was hosted by its first secretary, Henry O. Tallmadge, and attended by its first president Theodore Havemeyer. The next year Macdonald won the Amateur. The association flexed its muscles in that tournament by refusing to allow entrant Richard Peters to putt with a pool cue; and thereafter quickly established itself as the world's equipment authority. Its responsibility in that regard is in effect to this day.

The USGA quickly moved to ally itself with the R&A, the world's governing body. It soon became apparent that the two organizations would clash. While both were interested in the same goal—to protect, preserve and benefit the game—the difference in American and British cultures presented hurdles to be negotiated in the governing of golf. After more than century of operating with nearly, but not all, the same rules, the two authorities now abide by identical rulebooks.

As the popularity of golf soared in the U.S. over the first two decades of the 20th century, America began producing the majority of the world's best players. Until then, there is no question but that the golf elite had come from Britain. The American championships began attracting many of the top foreign players and the Yanks were traveling across the pond for the British events. The rivalry produced some terrific competition and ushered in a golden age for the game.

THE GOLDEN AGE

It was during the early 1920s that the golf professionals as a whole established decisive superiority in skill over the amateurs, and this superiority gradually earned them increasing respect among the game's governing bodies. Before that time, in America, most of the pros were Scottish immigrants who, whatever their skill, were (fairly or unfairly) best known for their love of a drink. Amateur golfers, and especially club committee members, who regarded golf as a game suitable only for the "better" class of citizen, had looked down on the pros—who were not even allowed to step into the clubhouse. The professional at that time was more often than not a former caddy—an occupation considered suitable only for the lower orders. Yet some of the greatest pros came up just this way: Walter Hagen, Sam Snead, Jimmy Demaret, Ben Hogan and Byron Nelson all were exposed to golf very early as bag carriers and club repairers. By contrast, golf's supreme amateur,

Bobby Jones, who never considered becoming a professional, was a Harvard-educated lawyer. Francis Ouimet, winner of the 1913 U.S. Open held at his local club at Brookline (Boston), was an exception to the rule. Ouimet was working as a caddy at the club when he beat the greatest golfer of the day, Britain's Harry Vardon; and the temptation to turn pro must have been extraordinary over the next few years. But Ouimet insisted on remaining an amateur, even when the USGA tried to rescind his status in 1917 after it discovered he was involved with a sporting-goods business.

There's a famous story about the flamboyant Walter Hagen at the 1920 British Open at Deal, in Kent. Hagen, upon learning he would not be allowed inside the clubhouse, hired a limousine to park right outside the front door and used his private transport as a luxurious locker room and cocktail bar. Hagen would become the first American-born player to win the British Open in 1922, and he won it again in 1924. The first U.S. Open at which pros were allowed inside the clubhouse was held at Inverness Club (Ohio) in 1920.

Hagen, along with his great rival Gene Sarazen, changed the way people looked at golf professionals in the United States. In Britain the Professional Golfers Association was formed in 1902. In 1916 the PGA of America was formed and now the pros had a voice. Today, the U.S. PGA represents nearly 24,000 men and women professionals around the country.

THE MASSES

Prosperity also had something to do with golf's growth through this era. The war was over and families had more money. More money meant more leisure time. Watching tournament golf became popular. The media fueled the game as well. Golf publications made stars out of the early heroes. British golfing legend Harry Vardon and fellow British star Ted Ray toured the States in 1913 and garnered much attention. Celebrities found golf attractive. Babe Ruth, Rosalind Russell and nearly every American president was swinging a club.

The Roaring 20s was a good time for golf and golf professionals. Tournament purses where increasing, relatively speaking, and there were events held in Florida, Texas and the West Coast. Tournament golf was spreading. The PGA TOUR was planting its seeds. By the mid-1920s, the total purse for all events was $77,000.

One man who would never see any of this money was the astonishing amateur Robert Tyre Jones, Jr. Jones was immensely popular. The World War II dampened golf's growth slightly. After the war, golf's new hero became the hardly comparable Ben Hogan. With the arrival of Arnold Palmer in the late 50s, golf was preparing for another huge boost.

MODERN HISTORY

The first televised golf event was the 1947 U.S. Open in St. Louis. Although it was partially shown and only locally, golf would never be the same again. In 1953 ABC televised the Tam O'Shanter Open (it cost promoters $32,000 to hire them) to a national audience estimated at two million. In that tournament, Lew Worsham holed a 135-yard wedge shot for an eagle to take the title from Chandler Harper. The drama of that shot turned a few network executive heads—and the race was on. Television contracts sent tournament purses skyrocketing.

No one was more poised to benefit from the hype than Arnold Palmer. With his rugged good looks, rapport with spectators and adventurous approach to the game, Palmer became golf's first visual-media darling. He attracted legions of fans that came to be known as "Arnie's Army." The list of exceptional players from 1960 to the present would consume pages. But the one man who towered over the game for most of that period was, of course, Jack Nicklaus.

Ever since the end of World War II the gap between the golf professional—that is, the chap who served you in the golf club shop and gave you golf lessons—and the professional (tour) golfer had been steadily widening. It had become feasible now to earn a living playing on tour. Many of the pros vying for top prizes had never worked in a pro shop. In the United States they had gone to college, where they had been involved in intensely competitive amateur events that served to equip them technically and temperamentally for life on the pro tour.

Recognizing the fortunes being reaped by the U.S. PGA from commercial sponsorships of events and through television revenues, the touring pros felt they should be better rewarded. But it was only in 1967, after the players threatened to start their own tour, that the PGA agreed to their demands. A Tournament Players Division was formed and given full rein to run its own competitions. In effect, of course, this created two distinct tiers of professional players—and the club pros were not pleased.

The European PGA Tour began in the early 1970s, and while it breeds world-class golfers and attracts great interest of its own, it remains in the shadow of the U.S. PGA Tour. Many of Europe's best golfers aspire to play in America to be tested by the best, not to mention get in on some of the much greater prize money on offer at U.S. tournaments.

As would be expected, there is tremendous competition to become a U.S. PGA Tour player. In 1965, the first PGA Tour Qualifying School was held at PGA National in Palm Beach Gardens, Florida. Would-be superstars must advance through excruciating regional events and the nerve-racking six-round final tournament to earn Tour cards. Many participants have expressed the conviction that there is more pressure in this competition than in many events on the Tour.

Ever-greater mountains of television money and sponsorship dollars continue to roll in. The first annual prize-money leader in professional golf was Paul Runyan with a 1934 take of $6,767. In the first four months of 1999, David Duval had already surpassed the record he set last year of nearly $2.5 million. Golf images are ever present now on television. In America, there is a 24-hour cable channel devoted to the sport. Office pools are run during major championships and there are even fantasy golf leagues. Golf equipment sales are astronomical and player-endorsement contracts obscene.

It's fair to say Old Tom Morris would be a wee bit surprised at what his game has wrought.

THE MAJORS

Golf's four major championships are The Masters, the United States Open, the British Open and the U.S. PGA Championship. How they became major championships, to be valued above all others, is a matter of debate. But there is not a golfer in the world, from the shaky beginner to the heroic hall-of-famer, that does not so consider them.

A golfer from any era does not achieve the accolade of true greatness unless he has outlasted the field in one or more major championships. The four tournaments are listed above in the order they're played. Previously, the British Amateur Championship and the United States Amateur had been regarded as majors, but as amateurs continued to falter in championships open to all comers, their major status was rescinded.

Only four players in the sport's history have won each of the majors at least once: Gene Sarazen (one Masters, two U.S., one British, three U.S. PGA); Ben Hogan (two Masters, four U.S., one British, two U.S. PGA); Gary Player (three Masters, one U.S., three British, two U.S. PGA); and Jack Nicklaus (six Masters, four U.S., three British, five U.S. PGA).

Writers have chronicled the epic struggles and triumphs of these tournaments in poem, in song, in essay and in film. The battles waged and careers made in these four competitions are permanent testimonials to their greatness.

THE MASTERS

The Masters has been played since 1934. It was originally called the Augusta Invitational Tournament after the course that it is always played upon—Augusta National in Georgia. It is the youngest major and the only one that does not and never has rotated venues. The tournament was the brainchild of the club's patriarch, Clifford Roberts, and its co-founder and most famous member, Bobby Jones. Jones' popularity—and his ability to attract the finest golfers, professional and amateur, who were numbered among his friends—is very likely the reason The Masters was catapulted to major status so quickly.

It is impossible to tell the story of The Masters without reviewing the background of its legendary club. In 1930 Jones retired from golf as the most successful amateur in history. That was the year, at age 28, Jones won all four of what were then considered golf's majors (British and U.S. Opens and Amateurs). He had always wanted to build a superior course far enough from his Atlanta home as to provide him a rare bit of privacy to play casual golf with friends. The ambitious Roberts, who shared Jones' desire and cherished their relationship, became the man responsible for raising the capital for the project—not an easy task with the United States already deep into the Depression. It's interesting to note that Roberts had trouble finding potential members willing to part with the $350-a-year fee.

MASTERS

1934	Horton Smith
1935	Gene Sarazen
1936	Horton Smith
1937	Byron Nelson
1938	Henry Picard
1939	Ralph Guldahl
1940	Jimmy Demaret
1941	Craig Wood
1942	Byron Nelson
1943	WWII
1944	WWII
1945	WWII
1946	Herman Keiser
1947	Jimmy Demaret
1948	Claude Harmon
1949	Sam Snead
1950	Jimmy Demaret
1951	Ben Hogan
1952	Sam Snead
1953	Ben Hogan
1954	Sam Snead

1955	Cary Middlecoff		1963	Jack Nicklaus
1956	Jack Burke, Jr.		1964	Arnold Palmer
1957	Doug Ford		1965	Jack Nicklaus
1958	Arnold Palmer		1966	Jack Nicklaus
1959	Art Wall, Jr.		1967	Gay Brewer, Jr.
1960	Arnold Palmer		1968	Bob Goalby
1961	Gary Player		1969	George Archer
1962	Arnold Palmer		1970	Billy Casper

WINNERS

1971	Charles Coody
1972	Jack Nicklaus
1973	Tommy Aaron
1974	Gary Player
1975	Jack Nicklaus
1976	Ray Floyd
1977	Tom Watson
1978	Gary Player
1979	Fuzzy Zoeller
1980	Seve Ballesteros
1981	Tom Watson
1982	Craig Stadler
1983	Seve Ballesteros
1984	Ben Crenshaw
1985	Bernhard Langer
1986	Jack Nicklaus
1987	Larry Mize
1988	Sandy Lyle
1989	Nick Faldo
1990	Nick Faldo
1991	Ian Woosnam
1992	Fred Couples
1993	Bernhard Langer
1994	José Maria Olazabal
1995	Ben Crenshaw
1996	Nick Faldo
1997	Tiger Woods
1998	Mark O'Meara
1999	José Maria Olazabal

Jones's personal relationship with the Scottish course architect (and retired physician) Dr Alister Mackenzie was critical in soliciting his services. Augusta National's early financial woes made paying the architect difficult, and in fact Mackenzie died before receiving his full fee. Mackenzie (already responsible for two of golf's greatest courses, Cypress Point in California and Royal Melbourne in Australia) designed a course to Jones' specifications on the site of a former horticultural nursery that was appealing both to the high-class player and golfing novice. Augusta National employs wide fairways and no rough. The fairway slopes make finding a level spot quite difficult. The greens are large but undulating and surrounded by trouble if the approach shots are wayward. The course's beauty—with its azaleas and dogwoods—is indescribable.

So it is here that The Masters takes place each spring. Originally, the tournament was by invitation only. It was important to Jones that the amateur golfer played a vital role at his tournament. It is still important to The Masters' organizers today. Roberts and Jones felt that it was also important to cater to the spectators—called patrons—so costs are kept low and crowds are kept small. In fact, the limited Masters gallery has been sold out for decades and the waiting list closed.

The competition for Masters glory has been legendary. Ever since Gene Sarazen, in 1935, holed out his second shot from about 220 yards on the par-5 15th hole to tie leader Craig Wood and go on to win the playoff, few of the tournaments have been less than dazzling. Nicklaus holds the record with six victories. Palmer has four. The big stars are normally involved in anxious battles that nearly always are decided on the back nine holes on the last day.

At tournament time, Augusta's greens are extremely firm and devilishly slick. It's not good enough to simply hit the greens in regulation; they must be hit in precise spots if the player is going to take two putts and walk off with a par. In 1999, in order to put a greater premium on accurate tee shots, the tournament committee narrowed the wide lawn-like fairways by having a slight cut of rough. This made it slightly more difficult to apply a totally predictable amount of spin to the ball on approach shots. However, a delicate putting touch is still the key to winning at Augusta.

THE UNITED STATES OPEN

The U.S. Open is the creation of the United States Golf Association. This mammoth organization, in addition to hosting various qualifying and championship tournaments, sets America's Rules of Golf, qualifies golf equipment as conforming or not and maintains the standards of handicap calculation that allow golfers of varying abilities to compete on an even field.

In 1895 the first U.S. Open was held at the Newport Golf Club, a 9-hole course in Rhode Island. It was a one-day, 36-hole event held in conjunction with the U.S. Amateur. It was considered less important than the Amateur at the time.

Professionals over from England and Scotland dominated the early Opens. Atlantic City's Johnny McDermott was the first American to triumph with his win at Chicago Golf Club—America's first 18-hole course—in 1911. Francis Ouimet won an 18-hole playoff over Harry Vardon and Ted Ray in 1913 at Brookline in Massachusetts. The victory was significant because Ouimet, a neighborhood kid who caddied at the course, was certainly not supposed to beat the great Brits. His triumph did much for the common golfer in America.

Perhaps the player most closely associated with the United States Open is Ben Hogan. Hogan won the tournament four times in six years (1948, 1950, 1951, 1953). More remarkable was Hogan's return from a near-fatal car accident in 1949 to recapture Open glory at Merion Golf Club, Philadelphia. America's first popular professional, Walter Hagen, won the first of his 11 Majors in the 1914 Open at Midlothian, Illinois. Nicklaus' first professional win was the 1962 U.S. Open at Oakmont. In one of the most famous shots in U.S. Open history, Tom Watson chipped in for an astonishing birdie on the short 17th to beat Nicklaus in 1982 at Pebble Beach, California.

A poll of U.S. PGA Tour players revealed the U.S. Open as the tournament they would most like to win. It's also the one dreamed about by most struggling amateur golfers. One way to play in the U.S. Open is to advance through one of the local and regional qualifying tournaments held by the USGA every year. It's an attainable—albeit extremely unlikely—goal.

The USGA is notorious for setting up its Open courses to ensure a severe test. The rough is grown to unimaginable heights while the greens are polished to a glassy finish. A player who ventures off the fairway is not expected to make birdie at the U.S. Open. The proponents of such mayhem believe America's supreme championship should take place on a course that penalizes a wayward shot. Opponents claim such a configuration rewards a too-safe approach. Regardless, there's no question the U.S. Open sets the stage for drama.

It is fitting here to offer a tribute to the winner of the 1999 U.S. Open, Payne Stewart, who died on October 25, 1999, at 42 years of age when the Learjet he was passenger on flew uncontrolled for hours before crashing in South Dakota. Stewart, known for his trademark knickers on tour, was on his way to Houston to participate in a PGA Tour championship.

THE BRITISH OPEN

This, the oldest and most internationally representative of the majors, began in 1860 at Prestwick links on Scotland's Ayrshire coast, where it was played for the first 12 years. Thereafter, until 1892, Prestwick alternated with St. Andrews and Musselburgh. That year, when Muirfield hosted, the championship was played over 72 holes for the first time (until then it had been over 36). The father and son of early golf's greatest family— Old Tom Morris and his boy Young Tom—dominated the initial tournaments. The Morrises took eight of the first 12 Open titles. Harry Vardon, golf's greatest player before World War I, is the career wins leader with six titles, his last coming in 1914 at Prestwick. British Open champions receive the coveted silver claret jug, first won by Young Tom Morris in 1872.

After a successful American run during the 1920s—with champions such as Hagen and Jones—hard economic times made transatlantic travel difficult and many of the Americans chose to stay home. The tournament was suspended from 1940-45 for World War II. All of this worked against the British Open, although Ben Hogan did win in 1953 at Carnoustie in his only British Open appearance. (He had already won the 1953 Masters and U.S.Open : nobody before or since has won three majors in a year; it is likely he would also have taken the U.S. PGA Championship that year if he had been able to get back to the United States in time after the British Open.)

Arnold Palmer is often credited with re-establishing the importance of the British Open as an international must-play. Palmer, who won back-to-back Opens in 1961 at Birkdale and 1962 at Troon, captivated the British golfing public just as he had the American. Arnie's success, and the emergence of television, made missing the Open inconceivable for the best golfers in the world.

Tom Watson has performed heroically in Britain as well. Watson, with five Open wins, established his legacy as a world-class player in this tournament. He set the 72-hole record at Turnberry in 1977 in a win over Nicklaus: they were paired together for the last two rounds in what is regarded as the greatest 36-hole head-to-head in the history of the majors.

Tony Jacklin became the toast of Britain with his win at Royal Lytham in 1969. The Spaniard Seve Ballesteros worked his magic at the Open and has three wins. The most recently celebrated Brit to succeed in the British Open is Nick Faldo, who had wins in 1987, 1990 and 1992.

The British Open, held in July, is always ripe for severe weather. The often windy and damp conditions force players to rely on imagination. Another unique aspect of the Open is the condition of the courses themselves. The limited-rotation venues provide classic links-style tracks not found anywhere else— St. Andrews, Muirfield, Turnberry, Troon, Birkdale, Lytham & St. Annes, and Royal St. George's (Sandwich); and, for 1999, the great shaggy monster of Carnoustie has been restored to favour. These courses are not the pristinely manicured target-style beauties normally played on the American PGA Tour. Players must contend with hidden bunkers, huge undulating greens and difficult lies. This, coupled with the tournament's unique tradition, makes the British Open a great occasion and a terrific event to watch: the champion is invariably a great player.

PGA CHAMPIONSHIP

When the PGA Championship was first held in 1916, amateur golfers were more popular—and most were better—than professional golfers. The pro of the time was just that: he worked in the golf shop, gave lessons and played competitively when he had time. With the lack of organized tournaments and prize money, it did not pay enough to be a professional golfer. Rodman Wanamaker, who was not a pro but a business man, recognized the plight of golf pros and set about organizing the Professional Golfers Association of America. The PGA of America runs the U.S. PGA Championship along with several other tournaments, including the Ryder Cup. The trophy won by the PGA champion is named for Wanamaker. The organization represents the thousands of golf pros around the country and oversees a good deal of the business of golf in the U.S.

The tournament itself began as a match-play event and remained so until 1958. This format appealed to players and fans and was probably scrapped at the behest of television executives. At its humble beginnings, it was not really considered a major. After early domination of the event by British professionals working in the U.S., the dashing American Walter Hagen owned the Wanamaker Trophy for four consecutive years from 1924 through 1927 (as well as in 1921.) The Haig, as well known for his match-play gamesmanship as his skills, took over from Gene Sarazen, who won the title in 1922 and 1923.

The 30s, 40s and 50s produced famous champions such as Paul Runyan (1934, 1938), Byron Nelson (1940, 1945), Sam Snead (1942, 1949, 1951) and Ben Hogan (1946, 1948). Jack Nicklaus won the event in three different decades, and Lee Trevino took the title in 1974 and 1984. The PGA Championship is the only major Arnold Palmer never won. John Daly won the 1991 PGA Championship at Crooked Stick after getting in the field as the ninth alternate. It was his first win as a professional. Paul Azinger was a popular winner at Inverness in 1993.

The PGA of America goes a long way to promote and protect golf in the U.S.; its fine tournament is indicative of the dedication and hard work of golf professionals everywhere.

THE ELITE

Debate rages over who were golf's greatest players, and it always will. In a game where tradition and history are treasured, it seems necessary to establish legends. How else will the rest be measured? While the argument surrounding the superstars from era to era will never be settled, four men are generally recognized as possessing the game and the temperament—and the sense of history—that puts them above all other golfers.

Bobby Jones

Robert Tyre Jones, Jr—"Bob" to his friends, "Bobby" to his fans and the media—embodied the "spirit of the game" in greater abundance than perhaps any other player in golf's history. Jones, a lifelong amateur, was singled out for his fairness, integrity and intolerance of anything that might impugn that spirit. And, to understate the point egregiously, Jones had game.

Jones' playing career was short. He played in only 52 official tournaments in a span of just over 14 years—but he won an astonishing 44 percent of them. Although contemporary professionals of the day had little opportunity to play against Jones (once yearly in each of the U.S. and British Opens), he was universally regarded as the best player in the world. There was no compelling reason for Jones to turn professional, as the big tournament money was yet to be available. He could be beaten on occasion, but no one ever beat Jones twice.

His greatest year, and arguably the greatest year any golfer has ever had, was 1930 when he became the only man to win what was then considered to be the Grand Slam—the U.S. Open, British Open, U.S. Amateur and British Amateur. (It's remarkable that even before 1930 Jones had collected nine victories in these tournaments.) He promptly retired from competitive golf, confessing that championship golf was by then taking an intolerable toll on his mental and emotional reserves.

Jones' post-championship career is compelling as well. With Clifford Roberts he established Augusta National Golf Club near his hometown of Atlanta. This course, regarded as one of the world's best, each year plays host to the first of golf's modern majors, The Masters.

Ben Hogan

Ben Hogan was not a natural. Hogan's insatiable work ethic and dedicated practice regimen only made it appear he was a

natural. This sweet-swinging Texan put in so much time on the range that some feel he invented golf practice. He didn't, of course, but he elevated it to an art form.

Hogan's early career was forgettable. He didn't win his first professional tournament until age 34 (1938 Hershey Fourball). Hogan foreshadowed his greatness in 1941 when he entered 39 tournaments and finished out of the top five only once. Then World War II hit.

Hogan picked right up after the war winning 21 times on Tour in the first two years back. His first victory in a major came in 1946 when he took the PGA Championship in Portland, Oregon. In 1948, Hogan put together the second longest streak in Tour history when he won six consecutive tournaments beginning with the U.S. Open at Riviera Country Club in Pacific Palisades, California.

Then in 1949 it all literally came crashing down. Hogan and his wife were in a horrible car accident and Ben smashed both of his legs. Doctors predicted he might never walk again. His return is the stuff of legend. He won two Masters (1951, 1953), three more U.S. Opens (1950, 1952, 1953) and a British Open (1953). Hogan's drive to perfect his golf swing allowed him to dominate the best players of his time. His commitment to continuing his dominance against all odds cemented his legendary status.

Arnold Palmer

Golf had been a popular game in the United States for a long time before Arnold Palmer. But Arnie is responsible for its outright explosion among the masses. With the benefit of nationwide television, Palmer became the people's champion spawning the ever present "Arnie's Army." This self-proclaimed battalion of fans was even known to kick a ball or two into a more fortuitous lie for the man who became known as "The King."

Palmer was from a small town (Latrobe, Pennsylvania) and had an effort-filled swing that more resembled those of his hacking admirers than most smooth passes made on Tour. He gave high-handicappers a reason to hope. He routinely expressed his wide array of emotions during play and the cameras were there to catch it all. He was and is adored.

Palmer's record speaks for itself. He had 60 victories on Tour, 91 worldwide and seven major titles. His victory total ranks fourth all time. Palmer owns the record for most Ryder Cup victories (22). He was named PGA Tour Player of the Year two times (1960 and 1962) and was the first to earn more than $1 million in a career. Palmer's business interests are thought to earn around $10 annually today.

But Palmer's career cannot be measured in wins and dollars. He played golf for the public and all that challenged him felt the weight of a nation against them. Palmer dueled in classic competitions against Hogan and Nicklaus and may just be the most popular figure in golf forever.

Jack Nicklaus

There never was a golfer who dominated the game as early, often or longer than did Jack Nicklaus. "The Golden Bear" was an outstanding amateur long before he earned his burly moniker. Nicklaus won two U.S. Amateur championships, the first at age 19. He was the U.S. collegiate champion at his beloved Ohio State University. His first professional win came in an 18-hole playoff victory over Arnold Palmer at Oakmont Country Club in 1962. The list goes on and on.

Nicklaus' greatest legacy is his performance in major championships. He seemed to be able to elevate his game in these most pressure-filled events and went on to capture 18 of them—the most ever. Nearly as remarkable is the number of majors he almost won. Nicklaus was famous for his last round comebacks in these and nearly every tournament he wasn't leading at the time. Nicklaus won his last major, The Masters, in 1986 at age 46. He is the oldest to capture a major title.

U.S. OPEN

1895	Horace Rawlins	1921	James Barnes
1896	James Foulis	1922	Gene Sarazen
1897	Joe Lloyd	1923	Bobby Jones
1898	Fred Herd	1924	Cyril Walker
1899	Willie Smith	1925	Willie MacFarlane
1900	Harry Vardon	1926	Bobby Jones
1901	Willie Anderson	1927	Tommy Armour
1902	Laurie Auchterlonie	1928	Johnny Farrell
1903	Willie Anderson	1929	Bobby Jones
1904	Willie Anderson	1930	Bobby Jones
1905	Willie Anderson	1931	Billy Burke
1906	Alex Smith	1932	Gene Sarazen
1907	Alex Ross	1933	Johnny Goodman
1908	Fred McLeod	1934	Olin Dutra
1909	George Sargent	1935	Sam Parks Jr.
1910	Alex Smith	1936	Tony Manero
1911	John McDermott	1937	Ralph Guldahl
1912	John McDermott	1938	Ralph Guldahl
1913	Francis Ouimet	1939	Byron Nelson
1914	Walter Hagen	1940	Lawson Little
1915	Jerome Travers	1941	Craig Wood
1916	Charles Evans Jr.	1942	WWII
1917	WWI	1943	WWII
1918	WWI	1944	WWII
1919	Walter Hagen	1945	WWII
1920	Edward Ray	1946	Lloyd Mangrum

WINNERS

1947	Lew Worsham		1973	Johnny Miller
1948	Ben Hogan		1974	Hale Irwin
1949	Cary Middlecoff		1975	Lou Graham
1950	Ben Hogan		1976	Jerry Pate
1951	Ben Hogan		1977	Hubert Green
1952	Julius Boros		1978	Andy North
1953	Ben Hogan		1979	Hale Irwin
1954	Ed Furgol		1980	Jack Nicklaus
1955	Jack Fleck		1981	David Graham
1956	Cary Middlecoff		1982	Tom Watson
1957	Dick Mayer		1983	Larry Nelson
1958	Tommy Bolt		1984	Fuzzy Zoeller
1959	Billy Casper		1985	Andy North
1960	Arnold Palmer		1986	Raymond Floyd
1961	Gene Littler		1987	Scott Simpson
1962	Jack Nicklaus		1988	Curtis Strange
1963	Julius Boros		1989	Curtis Strange
1964	Ken Venturi		1990	Hale Irwin
1965	Gary Player		1991	Payne Stewart
1966	Billy Casper		1992	Tom Kite
1967	Jack Nicklaus		1993	Lee Janzen
1968	Lee Trevino		1994	Ernie Els
1969	Orville Moody		1995	Corey Pavin
1970	Tony Jacklin		1996	Steve Jones
1971	Lee Trevino		1997	Ernie Els
1972	Jack Nicklaus		1998	Lee Janzen
			1999	Payne Stewart

Nicklaus in his prime played golf with an extremely powerful fade and was a tremendous driver of the ball. His length with the woods and irons was the envy of the Tour. His hunched-over putting style was reliably deadly. Nicklaus packaged all of these talents with an insatiable will to win and nerveless disposition. He was simply the best to ever play the game.

Since moving from the spotlight of the winner's circle, Nicklaus has established himself as one of the world's foremost golf course designers. His mark on the game is indelible and continues to spread.

THE GOLDEN CHAMPIONS

Old Tom Morris

Tom Morris, Sr., was the Jack Nicklaus of his day. That is from an involvement standpoint, Old Tom had his finger in just about everything. He was an outstanding player claiming four of the first eight British Opens ever played. He was a ball maker and club maker under the tutelage of links pioneer Allan Robertson. He is responsible for the design of many of the British Isles' first and most important golf courses—Carnoustie, Muirfield and Royal County Down among them. He was the greenskeeper at a course he first started playing at a very young age, St. Andrews, for many years. Old Tom was also the teacher of one of America's golf pioneers, C.B. Macdonald.

Young Tom Morris

A more dominant a golfer of the early age did not exist. Young Tom of course benefited from the tutelage of his father who instilled in him a solid all-around golf game and appreciation of it. Tommie was thought to be a prodigious driver and approach revolutionary. His short game was slick and he was known to be a master recovery artist. Young Tom won the British Open four times in a row (1868–72) and was the bane of fellow stars Willie and Mungo Park. Young Tom set the scoring record at the Open in 1870 and redefined how golf was played. He died of heartbreak at age 24 soon after his wife failed to survive the birth of the couple's baby.

Harry Vardon

Vardon has become the most famous member of Britain's "Great Triumvirate" along with J.H. Taylor and James Braid. He may endure more in the minds of historians because he won six British Open titles against five for the other two. He also won the United States Open in 1900 at Chicago Golf Club. Vardon is the namesake of the grip most used by golfers today although he didn't actually invent it. He did use it to perfection

as the basis for his markedly upright swing that produced high ballflight trajectory and supreme accuracy. As one of Britain's most well known professionals, Vardon made considerably more money giving golf exhibitions than he did for winning competitions.

James Braid

This Triumvirate member had the most success early on in the British Open reaching five titles before his counterparts did. This feat included back-to-back triumphs in 1905 at St. Andrews and 1906 at Muirfield. Braid did not swing as beautifully or powerfully as Vardon or Taylor but he was blessed with a superior putting touch. This is no small feat considering the condition of the greens at the turn of the century in Scotland. Braid became one of the foremost course designers of the era and laid out one of the world's first and greatest resort courses at Gleneagles, King's Course in 1919 in Perthshire.

John Henry Taylor

Taylor was born in the town of Northam very near Royal North Devon's Westward Ho! club where he learned the game at an early age. Taylor won the Open five times and in 1894 at Sandwich became the first non-Scotsman to do so. He employed a flat stroke producing a low ball ideally suited to keep his ball true in the wind. J.H. is as well known for his off-course efforts as he is for his outstanding golf ability. In 1901, he organized the first Professional Golfers' Association in response to club members circumventing the club pro's role when buying their equipment. His efforts have made him the patron saint of club professionals all over Europe.

Francis Ouimet

The precocious Ouimet propelled America's golf interest to new levels when he defeated the unbeatable Harry Vardon and fellow Englishman Ted Ray at The Country Club in the 1913 U.S. Open. Ouimet, a 20-year-old who lived in the Brookline, Massachusetts neighborhood of the Country Club and had caddied there, took the Brits to an 18-hole playoff where he won by five strokes. He was involved in a USGA controversy when he was stripped of his beloved amateur status having been discovered working at a sporting goods store in 1916. The public outcry led to USGA reinstating Ouimet one year later. Ouimet also won the U.S. Amateur in 1914.

Walter Hagen

Hagen is sometimes credited as the first full-time touring professional. He is always credited with a friendly demeanor and ability

to enjoy all the fruits available to him. He certainly was not a man an opponent wanted to play against as he was a gamesman of the highest order. Hagen won 11 major titles including a record six PGA Championships with a run of four consecutive (1924–27). In 1927, "The Haig" was captain of the first United States Ryder Cup team that beat Britain 9½ to 2½ signifying America's dominance of the game at the time. Hagen championed the rights of golf touring professionals and club professionals with equal vigor. After his competitive career faded, Hagen made a fine living touring the country giving exhibitions.

Gene Sarazen

Sarazen burst onto the golf scene early in life capturing two major titles (U.S. Open and PGA) in 1922 at the age of 20. With his goofy grip and diminutive stature, "The Squire" cut an odd figure on the course, but his success and influence on professional golf is undeniable. Sarazen's most famous shot, and possibly the most famous shot ever in golf, came in the 1935 Masters when he holed out for double eagle on the 15th hole to catch Craig Wood and win in a playoff. Sarazen went on to win seven major titles and was the first golfer to collect wins in all four majors. Sarazen was a bit of an equipment wizard as well and is the father of the sand wedge.

Tommy Armour

Somewhat overshadowed by the exploits of Hagen and Sarazen, "The Silver Scot" is still a beloved figure in golf. He is the winner of three major championships (1927 U.S. Open, 1930 PGA and 1931 British Open.) His U.S. Open win at Oakmont Country Club in Pennsylvania is a testament to the difficulty of American Open courses as he took the title with a 14-over-par score of 301 in a playoff. Armour fell from the scene when his putter became skittish with what Armour termed the "yips." This unfortunate condition and word remain part of the golfer's lexicon today. Armour was a teacher and instruction guru of considerable renown after his playing days.

THE CLASSIC CHAMPIONS

Sam Snead

Whatever technical aspects are applied to the golf swing, it remains an athletic maneuver involving rhythm and tempo. Snead may have had the most natural, athletic swing ever. It was a stroke that served "Slammin' Sammy" for a long time as he competed on Tour for nearly 30 years. Snead owns the career record for most wins on Tour with 81. He was victorious 135 times worldwide. One title that eluded him was the

U.S. Open although he was a three-time winner in the Masters and in the PGA Championship. Snead's lone British Open victory came at St. Andrews (1946) after he mistook the course as abandoned upon arrival.

Byron Nelson

Nelson owns a record on Tour that will never be broken. In 1945 he won 11 straight PGA Tour events and finished the year with 18. His earnings for the year were just more than $63,000 which was paid in war bonds. If Nelson had won at this rate in the 1998 PGA Tour season, his earnings would have topped $16 million. This amazing run took its toll on Nelson who retired after the 1946 season at the age of 34. It's frightening to think what he would have accomplished had he chosen to continue. As it was, Lord Byron won five majors.

Jimmy Demaret

Demaret loved Augusta National. The generous MacKenzie fairways and lack of rough was well suited to his favored fade. In the tournament's early years, Demaret was a big favorite of the Augusta galleries and he did not disappoint. From 1940 to 1950, Demaret won the green jacket three times (1940, 1947 and 1950). He actually posted a 30 on one trip through the back nine. The Texan was the first golfer to win three Masters titles—the only major title he was able to collect. The colorful Demaret was also well known for his gregarious personality and wild golf outfits.

Gene Littler

Littler enjoyed a considerably successful amateur career culminating in a United States Amateur title in 1953 in Oklahoma. In 1954, "Gene the Machine" surprised the golf world by winning a PGA Tour event as an amateur in his hometown San Diego Open. After turning professional, Littler went on to record 29 victories on Tour. His nickname stems from Littler's sweet natural swing that allowed him to repeat perfect passes at the ball time and time again. Littler repeated it under pressure in the 1961 U.S. Open at Oakland Hills to capture his only major. He represented the U.S. as a Ryder Cup team member seven times.

Gary Player

The South African Player was the first golfer and quite possibly one of the first athletes to sing the praises of a thorough fitness regimen and healthy diet. The dashing world traveler parlayed his routine into several major championships. He is one of only four players in history to have won all four majors. His 1978 Masters victory over Hubert Green, with a final round 64, is

one of the greatest comebacks in championship history. The strength of Player's golf game is his absolute mastery around the green. He is known also as one of golf's all-time great bunker players. Player is truly one of golf's most influential international ambassadors.

Lee Trevino

As an American Senior PGA Tour superstar today, fans love Trevino for his lively banter and cheeky disposition as they did his entire career. It was no fun for opponents however as Trevino chuckled his way to six major titles including two (U.S. Open and British Open) in 1971 and a successful defense of the British in 1972. Trevino, who was famous for honing his skills hustling around Texas, utilized his unorthodox swing to capture 27 titles on Tour and 27 more on the Senior Tour. "Supermex" was named PGA Tour Player of the Year in 1972.

Raymond Floyd

An extremely long career of top-level golf distinguishes Floyd as one of the game's greats. He is the only player other than

charismatic international star in golf. Seve's attraction lies partly in his totally fearless approach to the game, partly in one of the most graceful swings in golf, and partly in his affable yet intensely competitive personality: like Palmer, he wears his heart on his sleeve. He possesses one of the world's superior short games. His magical touch around the greens—he has chipped into the hole from light rough on countless important occasions—has put the seal of greatness on his game as a whole. His wizardry at escaping from all types of trouble is matched by his infectious joy in doing so. He has five major victories (three British Opens and two Masters), and in 1980 became the youngest man to don the green jacket at age 23.

Tom Watson

Watson is the winner of eight major championships including five British Opens. The only major to elude him is the PGA Championship. His Tour victory total stands at 33 as the ever-youthful Watson approaches 30 years on Tour. Watson's most famous shot came in the 1982 U.S. Open at Pebble Beach Golf Links in California. Trailing Jack Nicklaus by one heading into 17 on the last day, Watson left his approach behind the green. Facing a delicate shot to a green sloping away, the Kansas City native eased his chip onto the putting surface and it found the hole. He went on to win the championship.

Sam Snead to win a PGA Tour event in four different decades. Floyd has captured major titles on four different occasions (1969 PGA, 1976 Masters, 1982 PGA and 1986 U.S. Open.) His eight-stroke Masters win was one of the most dominant performances in the tournament's history. By winning the U.S. Open at age 44, he became the oldest player to do so. Floyd has taken his considerable skill onto the U.S. Senior Tour where he is one the competition's dominant players.

Severiano Ballesteros

From the late 70s to the early 90s, Ballesteros was the most

1860	Willie Park	1895	John H. Taylor
1861	Tom Morris, Sr.	1896	Harry Vardon
1862	Tom Morris, Sr	1897	Harold H. Hilton
1863	Willie Park	1898	Harry Vardon
1864	Tom Morris, Sr.,	1899	Harry Vardon
1865	Andrew Strath	1900	John H. Taylor
1866	Willie Park	1901	James Braid
1867	Tom Morris, Sr.	1902	Alexander Herd
1868	Tom Morris, Jr.	1903	Harry Vardon
1869	Tom Morris, Jr.	1904	Jack White
1870	Tom Morris, Jr.	1905	James Braid
1871	No Championship	1906	James Braid
1872	Tom Morris, Jr.	1907	Arnaud Massy
1873	Tom Kidd	1908	James Braid
1874	Mungo Park	1909	John H. Taylor
1875	Willie Park	1910	James Braid
1876	Bob Martin	1911	Harry Vardon
1877	Jamie Anderson	1912	Edward (Ted) Ray
1878	Jamie Anderson	1913	John H. Taylor
1879	Jamie Anderson	1914	Harry Vardon
1880	Robert Ferguson	1915	WWI
1881	Robert Ferguson	1916	WWI
1882	Robert Ferguson	1917	WWI
1883	Willie Fernie	1918	WWI
1884	Jack Simpson	1919	WWI
1885	Bob Martin	1920	George Duncan
1886	David Brown	1921	Jock Hutchison
1887	Willie Park, Jr.	1922	Walter Hagen
1888	Jack Burns	1923	Arthur G. Havers
1889	Willie Park, Jr	1924	Walter Hagen
1890	John Ball, Jr.	1925	James M. Barnes
1891	Hugh Kirkaldy	1926	Robert T. Jones, Jr
1892	Harold H. Hilton	1927	Robert T. Jones, Jr.
1893	William Auchterlonie	1928	Walter Hagen
1894	John H. Taylor	1929	Walter Hagen

1930	Robert T. Jones, Jr.	1965	Peter Thomson
1931	Tommy D. Armour	1966	Jack Nicklaus
1932	Gene Sarazen	1967	Roberto De Vicenzo
1933	Denny Shute	1968	Gary Player
1934	Henry Cotton	1969	Tony Jacklin
1935	Alfred Perry	1970	Jack Nicklaus
1936	Alfred Padgham	1971	Lee Trevino
1937	Henry Cotton	1972	Lee Trevino
1938	R. A. Whitcombe	1973	Tom Weiskopf
1939	Richard Burton	1974	Gary Player
1940	WWII	1975	Tom Watson
1941	WWII	1976	Johnny Miller
1942	WWII	1977	Tom Watson
1943	WWII	1978	Jack Nicklaus
1944	WWII	1979	Seve Ballesteros
1945	WWII	1980	Tom Watson
1946	Sam Snead	1981	Bill Rogers
1947	Fred Daly	1982	Tom Watson
1948	Henry Cotton	1983	Tom Watson
1949	Bobby Locke	1984	Seve Ballesteros
1950	Bobby Locke	1985	Sandy Lyle
1951	Max Faulkner	1986	Greg Norman
1952	Bobby Locke	1987	Nick Faldo
1953	Ben Hogan	1988	Seve Ballesteros
1954	Peter Thomson	1989	Mark Calcavecchia
1955	Peter Thomson	1990	Nick Faldo
1956	Peter Thomson	1991	Ian Baker-Finch
1957	Bobby Locke	1992	Nick Faldo
1958	Peter Thomson	1993	Greg Norman
1959	Gary Player	1994	Nick Price
1960	Kel Nagle	1995	John Daly
1961	Arnold Palmer	1996	Tom Lehman
1962	Arnold Palmer	1997	Justin Leonard
1963	Bob Charles	1998	Mark O'Meara
1964	Tony Lema	1999	Paul Lawrie

Bottom & Right: Greg Norman, 1997 Dubai Desert Classic

Below right: Fred Couples, 1999 U.S. Masters, Augasta National

Below: Nick Faldo, 1993 British Open, Royal St. George's

THE MODERN CHAMPIONS

Nick Faldo

Elite professional golfers normally start playing the game very early in life and develop solid swings that carry them to the upper echelons. Nick Faldo didn't pick up a golf club until age 14 and did develop a terrific golf swing. But after considerable success in Europe, the Englishman decided to completely over-haul his swing in the mid-80s believing the one he had been playing with was lacking. Apparently his dedication paid off as he has gone on to capture six major titles (three British Opens and three Masters) including back to back green jackets in 1989–90. Faldo is the best English golfer of many decades and is a beloved figure at home and around the world.

Greg Norman

Globetrotting is the norm for this dashing Australian. Winner of 73 tournaments worldwide, "The Shark" has parlayed his success into many millions. He has won golf tournaments in no less than 13 different countries. He was the first player to sur-pass $10 million in career earnings on the American PGA Tour. Norman has won two British Open titles (1986 Turnberry, 1993 Royal St. George's) But he may be known even more for the number of times he has been close to winning majors. He has been runner up in eight championships including the wrong end of four playoffs. Norman was the sentimental favorite in the 1999 Masters where he came off surgery to place a remarkable third.

Nick Price

A leader of the current crop of international superstars, Price had one of the greatest years ever on the American PGA Tour when he captured six victories in 1994. Included among those are two major titles (British Open at Turnberry and PGA at Southern Hills). He was named PGA Tour Player of the Year in that campaign. Price is universally regarded as one of the most pleasant players in the world. The Zimbabwe native employs a very compact, athletic swing that he is able to rely upon in pressure situations. Reeling from the attention of such a phenomenal '94, Price faltered in 1995 and '96 and failed to win a tournament. He rebounded in 1997 and is again in con-tention.

Fred Couples

Always a fan favorite, Couples was voted PGA Tour Player of the Year in 1991 and 1992. The 1992 campaign was an extremely successful one that saw the American win the

Masters. That victory capped off a run of three wins and two seconds in six starts. His $1.3 million dollar take that year was tops on Tour. Couples has represented the United States five times in Ryder Cup competition and has never missed a cut at Augusta National. Freddie suffered through considerable back problems during the middle '90s but has recovered to again contend as one of the best players in the world. Couples' effortless swing has allowed him to capture 17 title worldwide.

Mark O'Meara

In 1981, O'Meara was the PGA Tour's Rookie of the Year. Currently, at age 42, O'Meara is enjoying the greatest amount of success of his entire career. In 1998, he won two majors (Masters, British Open at Royal Birkdale) and went on to become PGA Tour Player of the Year. His Masters win, after 15 trips to Augusta, came in dramatic fashion. He finished birdie-birdie to barely beat two current Tour stars, David Duval and Fred Couples. O'Meara has enjoyed his time on the Monterey Peninsula winning the Pebble Beach Pro-Am a record five times and has 23 victories worldwide. He has played on five American Ryder Cup teams.

Davis Love III

For several seasons, Love carried the albatross of being the "best player never to win a major." Consistently near the leaders, he just couldn't seem to reach the top. That all changed in 1997 when Love bested the field by five strokes in the PGA Championship at Winged Foot Country Club in New York. His walk up 18 on the final day as a rainbow burst through the clouds is one of golf's most enduring images. Love placed second in the 1999 Masters continuing his impressive record of placing in the top 20 in 11 of 17 majors entered. Noted for his incredible length off the tee, Love is also one of the American PGA Tour's most accurate.

Left & Right: Tiger Woods, Johnny Walker Classic, Thailand, January 25, 1998

Below Left: Ernie Els, 1999 Alfred Dunhill PGA Championship, Johannesburg South Africa

Below Right: David Duval, 1999 Players Championship, TPC at Sawgrass, Penote Vedra Beach

Ernie Els

A stunning image of golfer as athlete, the South African Els grew up a multi-sport star. Early successes in tennis and rugby gave way to his golf prowess at age 14. Els burst upon the American golf scene in 1994 with a United States Open win at Oakmont Country Club in Pennsylvania. Steady play kept him near the top for the next few years and then he repeated his Open win in 1997 with a victory at Congressional CC in Maryland. With this triumph, Els became the first foreign player to win two U.S. Opens since Alex Smith in 1906 and 1910. Always in major contention, the burly Els is expected to collect many more titles in the future.

David Duval

In the current era of international golf stars, the American Duval is universally considered the best. In 1998 he set a PGA Tour earnings record of nearly $2.6 million notching four wins. The 1999 season began promisingly as Duval recorded four wins in the first two months, already eclipsing 1998's earnings record. With a season scoring average of less than 69, it is quite apparent, Duval utilizes his superior skills to the utmost. He is also well known for his unflappable course demeanor. Duval put together one of the finest rounds in Tour history at the 1999 Bob Hope Chrysler Classic when he posted a 59. His score tied the lowest ever shot on Tour and became the lowest score ever recorded in a final round.

Eldrick "Tiger" Woods

No golfer has ever made as trumpeted an entrance onto the PGA Tour as Tiger Woods in 1996—and for good reason. Only Bobby Jones surpasses Woods' amateur career. At the age of 15, he won the first of three consecutive U.S. Junior Amateur titles. In 1994, he became the youngest player to win the U.S. Amateur title and then won it the two years following. In 1996, he added the U.S. NCAA championship. When Woods turned professional, corporations clamored for his services and he gathered some $100 million in long-term endorsement contracts.

His sponsors were rewarded handsomely when Woods won the 1997 Masters. His 12-stroke margin of victory is the largest in tournament history and his 18-under-par 270 shattered the tournament record. He also became the youngest player ever to win a green jacket at the age of 21 years, 3 months.

GREAT COURSES

It's impossible obviously to highlight every elegant course worthy of such attention. Golf magazines around the world make a lot of noise with their issues devoted to the completely inexact practice of rating the great tracks. There are countless fantastic ways where and how to string together a set of golf holes and they're all wonderful in their own right. Experiencing the designer's vision is part of the beauty of playing golf. Absorbing the history of spike marks long mowed over is another.

EARLY BRITISH COURSES

As might be imagined, the five courses featured here hearken back to a time when the sea, the wind and the rain shaped much of the layout. Grazing sheep did most of course maintenance, and players excelled at low bump-and-run shots.

St. Andrews, Old Course

Address: St. Andrews, Fife, Scotland • Architect: Unknown
Established: 1552 (first licence issued for golf
and other sports)

The first time Sam Snead came to the Old Course, he thought he'd stumbled upon a golf links long out of use. Such is the rugged, treeless beauty of St. Andrews—generally accepted as the home of golf. While the 6,933-yard, par-72 layout itself is not particularly difficult for modern-day professionals, the wind that so often blows over the best British links can make the Old Course devilish at best and impossible at worst. Its bunkers are legendary—the deep, vertical-faced greenside bunker on the great 17th Road Hole has humbled would-be champions for decades.

Originally 22 holes, the Old Course was reduced to 18, establishing the norm for golf courses throughout the world. Golfers play nine away from the historic clubhouse, and the back nine shoots back again in classic links style. The layout is singular in that on 14 holes there is a double green: half of each of these immense, undulating greens is for a hole on the outward nine, the other half for a hole on the back nine. Golfers are troubled by many blind shots and small but deep pot bunkers. St. Andrews Old Course requires mastery of the wind and a deft short game.

The British Open has been staged here more than 20 times producing such great champions as J.H. Taylor (1895, 1900), Bobby Jones (1927), Snead (1946), Jack Nicklaus (1970, 1978), and Seve Ballesteros (1984).

Carnoustie

Address: Angus, Scotland • Architect: Allan Robertson; later,
Tom Morris; redesigned by James Braid (1926)
Established: 1842

Scottish golf pioneer Allan Robertson set Carnoustie's original 10 holes over the ruddy heathlands of his country's east coast. Old Tom Morris updated the course to 18 holes a quarter century later. In the 1920s British champion James Braid gave Carnoustie another shine by replacing the tees and greens. He also added new bunkers. The course is widely accepted as one of Scotland's toughest golf tests at 6,941 yards from the tips. When the wind is up, as it normally is, survival is the goal.

Carnoustie's final holes are called the "Sting-in-the-Tail" for good reason. Sixteen is a frightening 250-yard par-3 with an elevated green rejecting all but the most precise tee shots. The Barry Burn meanders across the 17th fairway at three points. Number 18 is a 486-yard scorpion on which the Barry Burn comes in to play twice more.

The Open returned to Carnoustie in 1999 for the first time since 1975, when Tom Watson won in an '18-hole playoff to establish his reputation as an international star. Ben Hogan won here with a magisterial final round in 1953 in his only British Open appearance. Tommy Armour (1931), Henry Cotton (1937) and Gary Player (1968, when he bested Jack Nicklaus) were also Open champions at Carnoustie.

Royal Liverpool (Hoylake)

Address: Hoylake, Merseyside, England
Architect: Robert Chambers and George Morris
Established: 1869

Hoylake is built on the site of a former racetrack along the sea. For a long time it was used for golf and racing. At first glance, Royal Liverpool Golf Club appears to pose a fairly routine challenge to the skilful golfer. As they say, appearances can be deceiving, and the truth is that Hoylake is one of the sternest tests in England, if not all the British Isles. The course can be run out to nearly 7,000 yards. But the real difficulty lies, as it often does, with the wayward shot. A good deal of the course is bordered by out-of-bounds terrain, so that even the slightest miscue or miscalculation can prove extremely costly. This is especially true at the 17th green where a difficult approach must hold for fear of the OB road running behind. A shot too tentative is likely to find the bunkers fronting the green. The greens themselves have a reputation for excellence and course maintenance in general is top notch.

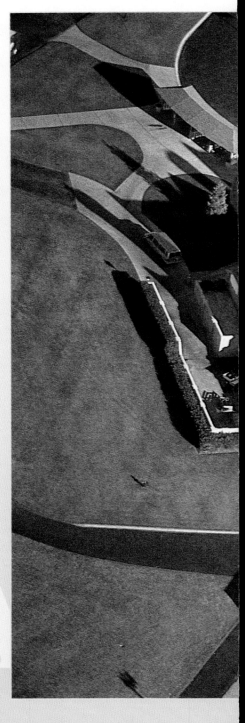

1916	James A. Barnes		1958	Dow Finsterwald
1917	WWI		1959	Bob Rosburg
1918	WWI		1960	Jay Hebert
1919	James A. Barnes		1961	Jerry Barber
1920	Jock Hutchinson		1962	Gary Player
1921	Walter Hagen		1963	Jack Nicklaus
1922	Gene Sarazen		1964	Bobby Nichols
1923	Gene Sarazen		1965	Dave Marr
1924	Walter Hagen		1966	Al Geiberger
1925	Walter Hagen		1967	Don January
1926	Walter Hagen		1968	Julius Boros
1927	Walter Hagen		1969	Raymond Floyd
1928	Leo Diegel		1970	Dave Stockton
1929	Leo Diegel		1971	Jack Nicklaus
1930	Tommy Armour		1972	Gary Player
1931	Tom Creavy		1973	Jack Nicklaus
1932	Olin Dutra		1974	Lee Trevino
1933	Gene Sarazen		1975	Jack Nicklaus
1934	Paul Runyon		1976	Dave Stockton
1935	Johnny Revolta		1977	Lanny Wadkins
1936	Denny Shute		1978	John Mahaffey
1937	Denny Shute		1979	David Graham
1938	Paul Runyon		1980	Jack Nicklaus
1939	Henry Picard		1981	Larry Nelson
1940	Byron Nelson		1982	Raymond Floyd
1941	Vic Ghezzi		1983	Hal Sutton
1942	Sam Snead		1984	Lee Trevino
1943	WWII		1985	Hubert Green
1944	Bob Hamilton		1986	Bob Tway
1945	Byron Nelson		1987	Larry Nelson
1946	Ben Hogan		1988	Jeff Sluman
1947	Jim Ferrier		1989	Payne Stewart
1948	Ben Hogan		1990	Wayne Grady
1949	Sam Snead		1991	John Daly
1950	Chandler Harper		1992	Nick Price
1951	Sam Snead		1993	Paul Azinger
1952	Jim Turnesa		1994	Nick Price
1953	Walter Burkemo		1995	Steve Elkington
1954	Chick Harbert		1996	Mark Brooks
1955	Doug Ford		1997	Davis Love III
1956	Jack Burke		1998	Vijay Singh
1957	Lionel Hebert			

ONSHIP
WINNERS

Hoylake was the site of the first British Amateur championship and where Bobby Jones won the third leg (British Open) of his 1930 Grand Slam. It has hosted 10 Opens over the years, the last in 1967. In 1921 it was the venue for the first team competition between Britain and the United States, an event that inspired the inaugural Walker Cup in 1922.

Royal St. George's
Address: Sandwich, Kent, England
Architect: Dr. W. Laidlaw Purves
Established: 1887

The creation of Royal St. George's involved a bit of heavenly intervention. Dr W.L. Purves, after searching about for land for his golf course, is said to have spotted the area for St. George's from a Sandwich church tower. The reliability of golf tales being what they are—especially those passed down over many generations—there's no telling if this event actually took place. It requires no leap of faith, however, to call Royal St. George's a divine course.

Purves was the original architect. The man many consider the top architect ever, Scotsman Alister Mackenzie, remodeled the course. Designer Frank Pennink had a go in the 1970s.

Royal St. George's sits hard against Pegwell Bay to the north of Dover in Kent. It is interesting in many respects, not the least of which is the encroachment of the watery thoroughfare known as the Suez Canal that runs through the 14th hole. One of its most diifficult holes is the 470-yard, par-4 4th. Aside from the sheer length of the hole, players must carry a gigantic bunker that slopes against nearly 70 degrees. It's not a difficult hazard to get over from the tee but it's a devil to escape from.

It was the first course outside Scotland to host the British Open when J.H.Taylor won in 1894. It has hosted the championship 10 times since, its greatest winners including Harry Vardon (1899 and 1911), Walter Hagen (1922 and 1928), Henry Cotton (1934), the great South African Bobby Locke (1949), and Greg Norman (1993).

Muirfield
Address: Gullane, East Lothian, Scotland
Architect: Old Tom Morris and Harry Colt
Established: 1891

Britain's first organized club The Honourable Company of Edinburgh Golfers began its odyssey in Leith, moved on to Musselburgh and finally settled here at Muirfield. The course claims several designers, the first Old Tom Morris of St.

Andrews. Morris' work was of the most basic plotting and David Plenderleith refined the course shortly thereafter. The work of Harry Colt remains most associated with the design of Muirfield today although Tom Simpson and Henry Maxwell took their redesign turns as well.

The 6,941-yard, par-72 course has been placed solidly among the top tracks in the world. Its reputation for requiring difficult but fair golf shots has made Muirfield a favorite British Open course for top professionals old and new.

This lowland links course follows gently the soft rolls of the natural terrain on the southern shore of the Firth of Forth, east of Edinburgh. It is known for its dastardly par-3s, all of which feature small, slick and elevated greens. As Nick Faldo pointed out in 1987, long approach shots are welcomed by generous greens and shortish approach shots must hit small targets. Faldo won the tournament that year and again in 1992. Other notable Open winners at Muirfield include Walter Hagen (1929), Henry Cotton (1948), Gary Player (1959), Jack Nicklaus (1966), Lee Trevino (1972), and Tom Watson (1980).

BRITAIN, POST-1900

While most of the following courses are also quite early, it's impossible to ignore the wealth of design tradition that Britain has enjoyed for a long time.

Sunningdale
Address: Sunningdale, Surrey, England • Architect: Willie Park
Established: 1901

When British champion Willie Park got his hands on the land to become Sunningdale, he was faced with a lovely but relatively unimaginative collection of farms owned by Cambridge. The original layout was a parkland design. Harry Colt, secretary of the club for nearly 20 years, took hold of it and went about planting trees throughout the course. What resulted was a fabulous collection of holes each secluded from the rest. A round at Sunningdale is peaceful and extremely enjoyable—until you come to the 18th. Eighteen at Sunningdale's old course is a long par-4 requiring a big drive uphill to a landing area flanked on right and left by fairway bunkers. The target on the lengthy approach is the club's signature massive oak tree and clubhouse.

The tee box on the 10th hole is a wondrous place. The most elevated point on the course, the par-5 provides a breathtaking view of the English countryside. From there, it's a downhill drive that, if struck well enough, presents the opportunity to reach the green in two.

A unique aspect of the course is its two opening holes—both par-5s. While Sunningdale never has held the British Open, it has played host to the Walker Cup and several Open qualifying tournaments.

Turnberry

Address: Ayrshire, Scotland • Architect: Willie Fernie
Established: 1903

The verses devoted to the countryside surrounding Turnberry are legendary. Writers, including local Robert Burns, have sung wistfully the praises of the River Clyde and the Isle of Arran and they just as poetically could have written about Turnberry's Ailsa course. The original course, named for landmark Ailsa Craig (a vast plug of volcanic rock that rears out of the Firth of Clyde), hugs the seaside in classic Scottish links fashion. The largest thrill comes near the turn where the 9th hole is guarded by Turnberry's unmistakable lighthouse. The tee box here at Bruce's Castle, a 454-yard par-4, is set upon a ledge among the cliffs over Turnberry Bay. The tee ball must carry a portion of the inlet below.

It's not possible to discuss Turnberry without mentioning the phenomenal Turnberry Hotel. Built in 1906, the luxury property is perched upon a hill with spectacular views of the Firth of Clyde. The clubhouse recently underwent a complete overhaul and the hotel features a terrific spa.

Open competition at Turnberry has been no less tantalizing. The first here, 1977, was won by Tom Watson who set the tournament scoring record with a 268, just one shot ahead of Jack Nicklaus. Greg Norman was victorious in 1986, and Nick Price won in 1994 by one stroke.

Gleneagles, King's Course
Address: Auchterarder, Perthshire, Scotland
Architect: James Braid
Established: 1919

The Gleneagles Hotel is a golf destination of the highest quality. The facility boasts four courses, including Jack Nicklaus' new Monarch 18 and the 9-hole "Wee Course." The hotel caters admirably to the golf traveler, and the instructional school and practice facilities are first rate. But the King's course is the jewel.

The King's is not overwhelmingly treacherous. But a command of iron distance and shot selection is paramount. This becomes apparent right away with the approach to the first green. A benign uphill 350-yarder that should be made short with a good drive, the hole always plays longer than expected and a large number of first-timers end up in the front bunker 20 feet below the green.

The scenery about this inland course is stunning. Craggy mountain peaks loom northward while rolling green hills fall away to the south—and that is where putts normally follow.

Gleneagles has not hosted the British major but has been home to the European Tour's Scottish Open. After playing the course, the inimitable Lee Trevino quipped, "If heaven is as good as this, I sure hope they have some tee times left."

Wentworth
Address: Virginia Water, Surrey, England
Architect: Harry Colt
Established: 1924

The West course at Wentworth is a stern test of golf for the seasoned veteran yet an enjoyable experience for the novice playing from the less taxing forward tees. In 1924 Harry Colt, former secretary of nearby Sunningdale, had by this time turned all his attention to golf course design, and he erected two courses in this attractive estate set among woods and heathland. Colt stretched his West course—known today as the Burma Road—to nearly 7,000 yards.

Accurate driving and iron play is the only way to get around this course. Course management is also essential to

success, especially at the 466-yard 15th, a long and subtle par 4. The hole demands a well placed drive of some distance. A ditch runs diagonally across the fairway, forcing the player to decide exactly how much to cut off. The 17th is no English tea either. The 571-yard par-5 is long even by professional standards. A gentle dogleg left, bounded by trees at left (out of bounds) and right, its fairway slopes to the right in the landing area of the necessarily long drive, and all but the finest controlled draw ends up in the right-hand rough.

Wentworth hosted the first professional team competition between Britain and the United States. These matches inspired the inauguration of the Ryder Cup, which the club also hosted in 1953. Today it plays host to the World Matchplay Championship every autumn.

Loch Lomond
Address: Loch Lomond, Luss, Scotland
Architect: Tom Weiskopf and Jay Morrish
Established: 1994

A creek runs along the left, forming a pond behind the green. The lone respite is the generous proportions of the green.

The course does not possess the centuries-old tradition of many of its Scottish brethren but it is certain to establish a tradition of its own.

EARLY UNITED STATES

The first United States courses began just as the first Scottish tracks. Holes were configured with the lay of the land. Early American golfers played in pastures, fields and orchards. It was not long however before horses and earth-moving equipment were toppling trees, altering hills and carving mountains—always, of course, with an eye toward preserving as much of the natural terrain as possible. What resulted is a collection of amazing golf courses that are uniquely American.

Pine Valley Golf Club
Address: Clementon, New Jersey
Architects: George Crump and Harry Colt
Established: 1919

The driving force behind Pine Valley, George Crump, didn't live to see his vision—some would call it his nightmare—to completion. With just 14 holes finished, Crump went to the big bunker in the sky and Harry Colt, along with the Wilson brothers finished the project.

Pine Valley is built on a 184-acre bunker covered with thick underbrush, oaks and of course pines. The sandy soil produces brilliant turf on the fairways. The natural ground cover and trees establish a phenomenal setting for golf. Pine Valley is considered one of toughest, if not the toughest, courses in the world. It measures 6,765 yards from the tips with a par of 70. Long indeed, but the most intimidating facet of Pine Valley is that the tees, landing areas and greens are the only areas accepting of a golf ball. There is no room for error. The first par-5 on the course measures 585 yards with a carry known as "Hell's Half Acre." The other par-5 is the 603-yard 16th. Despite the difficulty, Pine Valley is considered by many to be among the finest anywhere.

Pebble Beach Golf Links
Address: Pebble Beach, California
Architects: Jack Neville and Douglas Grant
Established: 1919

Coastal golf does not get much better the heavenly 18 strung upon the cliffs of Monterey in central California. Designer Jack

The youngster of the group, Loch Lomond is the work of what many consider America's premier design team of the moment. Weiskopf has said he considers this course his most inspirational work to date. The parkland layout spreads about the historic Clan Colquhoun estate on the banks of Loch Lomond, the largest landlocked lake in the British Isles. Although the course has been open only a few years, there is a distinctly historical atmosphere.

There is also a distinctly intimidating atmosphere for all but the best golfers on top of their game around the 7060-yard, par-71 course. The intimidation begins when one looks at the scorecard to discover that the par-5 sixth hole measures no less than 625 yards. Even for the professionals, this is a three-shot hole. It is the longest in Scotland, and the loch runs down the entire right side. The fairway houses a menacing cross-bunker that forces a multitude of decisions. To top it all off, the green is among the smallest on the course.

The 455-yard, par-4 10th hole is as beautiful as it is demanding. There is no room for error in the elevated tee shot.

Neville, a five-time California Amateur champion, recognized the astonishing setting he had to work with, "The golf course was there all the time. All I did was find the holes."

Mature Monterey Pines squat windswept along the cliffs. Steep canyons await wayward shots, as does the Pacific Ocean that runs along eight holes on this 6,799-yard, par-72 adventure. Each hole, with its stunning beauty, is capable of lulling the golfer into a duffing dream state. A rude awakening waits however on the two finishing holes. The 17th is a 209-yard par-3 that consistently plays into a prevailing wind. The salty air is coming off the sea that serves as a backdrop for the green. The putting surface is an hourglass shape that, depending on the pin placement and approach shot, is liable to require a lay-up putt. Eighteen at Pebble Beach is a home hole of utter grandeur. The 548-yard par-5 is not reachable in two. The Pacific runs along the left for the entire length of the hole. The fabulous green complex sits hard against The Lodge—perhaps the most envied golf resort in America.

Cypress Point Golf Club

Address: Pebble Beach, California
Architect: Alister MacKenzie
Established: 1928

Cypress Point has been described as the most picturesque, awe-inspiring golf course in the world. It also very well may be the most exclusive club on the planet. Those lucky enough to have experienced the cliffs and ocean canyons of Cypress Point claim there are more deer roaming the fairways than golfers.

The name of the course is derived from the ancient Monterey Cypress trees that dot the course in their gnarled splendor. The 6,536-yard, par-72 collection plays inland for the first 13 holes. As it emerges oceanward at 14, the breath is taken away.

The 143-yard, par-3 15th is played to a green seemingly set in the sea. Waves crash loudly against the craggy rocks nearly drowning out the barks of sea lions that call them home. Number 16 is a par-3 in name only. At 231 yards, the green is accessible only to the bravest swingers. The hole is nearly all carry over the Pacific save the bailout area that most score-conscious golfers are advised to take. Seventeen is a 393-yard par-4 with a green that requires pinpoint accuracy. Falling off into the ocean and guarded by bunkers on the left and back left, the 17th green is as gorgeous as it is unfriendly. Interestingly, the 18th hole is considered supremely anti-climactic.

Below: 13th green Augusta National, Georgia

Shinnecock Hills Golf Club

Address: Southhampton, New York
Architects: Howard Toomey and William S. Flynn
Established: 1891

The architect of Shinnecock's first 12 holes was actually Scotsman Willie Dunn who made the trip at the behest of America's richest golf nut at the time William K. Vanderbilt. Dunn served as the club's professional for several years. He gathered more than 100 Shinnecock Indians for labor and set about laying out one of the oldest clubs in the United States. His Long Island work was followed up later by Howard Toomey and William Flynn.

Shinnecock Hills is not terribly forgiving of the wayward shot. Fairways are narrow and several cuts of rough extend out from its edges culminating in the snarly native fescue that is known to swallow golf balls and engulf clubheads.

Shinnecock plays 6,980 yards from the tips and incorporates a number of strategically placed bunkers but little water. The club was the first in America to be incorporated and the first to construct a clubhouse. Stanford White brilliantly designed the structure.

Shinnecock Hills hosted the second ever U.S. Open in 1895 and didn't entertain another until Raymond Floyd's 1986 victory. In 1995, the USGA returned to Shinnecock—one of the organization's founding members—to play its centennial tournament won by Corey Pavin.

Augusta National

Address: Augusta, Georgia
Architects: Alister MacKenzie and Bobby Jones
Established: 1933

Augusta National is known to the masses as the home of the Masters. Each April the exclusive membership opens its doors to the public to stage what many consider golf's finest tournament. But back in 1933, it was famous because it was the club of Bobby Jones. Jones' popularity as the greatest golfer of many generations and a true gentleman is what enabled Clifford Roberts to gather the funds to build the club and what immediately established the Masters as a top-tier event—indeed instantly a Major Tournament.

The layout itself is not a demanding one. Jones and designer Alister MacKenzie agreed that the membership should have a beautiful, enjoyable course to play that would not leave them feeling dejected. The glorious flora and soft undulating fairways are testament to their success.

The course can be difficult. At tournament time, the greens are maddeningly slick. An azalea is not as pretty when it's hiding a golf ball. Hazards such as Rae's Creek will come into play. The tournament committee left a slight cut of rough alongside the fairway in 1999 for the first time.

Augusta is an overwhelming favorite among golf fans as they feel they know the course from seeing it on television for so many years. And it is worthy of all praise thrown its way.

LATER UNITED STATES

As construction equipment advanced and more money came into the game, American course builders pushed forward to generate an amazing number of quality courses. They discovered new turf technology and superior irrigation systems that allowed them to access a level of design philosophy unmatched worldwide.

Muirfield Village Golf Club
Address: Dublin, Ohio
Architects: Jack Nicklaus and Desmond Muirhead
Established: 1974

Muirfield Village is Jack Nicklaus' course just as Augusta is Jones' and Bay Hill is Arnold Palmer's. One reason it's so popular among players and course raters is its association with the greatest player the game has known. Another reason is because it is a superb golf course.

During the PGA Tour's Memorial Tournament, the course stretches out to 7,163 ornery yards. There are nearly 70 bunkers strategically placed throughout and water comes into play on 11 holes. The course is always in superb condition during golf season.

In 1966, Nicklaus won his first British Open. The victory came at Muirfield in East Lothian, Scotland. Scottish observers felt Nicklaus enjoyed the course—and no doubt his victory—so much that he flew home and built Muirfield Village. The 220-acres housing Muirfield Village was purchased in 1966, but Jack didn't get around to building the course until 1972.

The Memorial Tournament attracts a top field each year. Nicklaus has won the event twice since its inception (1977 and 1984). Other past champions include Tom Watson (1979 and 1996), Raymond Floyd (1982), Greg Norman (1990 and 1995) and Tom Lehman (1994).

TPC at Sawgrass
Address: Ponte Vedra Beach, Florida • Architect: Pete Dye
Established: 1980

Pete Dye has established himself as one of America's premier course architects of the last 30 years. His designs challenge players of all abilities and TPC at Sawgrass is no exception. While some find Dye's incessant use of railroad ties and other such unnatural gimmicks tiresome, there's no question his reputation for greatness is firmly set.

Water hazards are prevalent on most holes at Sawgrass—a hazard often found in abundance on Mr. Dye's

layouts. Another typical Dye hazard, waste bunkers, make their presence felt strongly throughout the design. TPC at Sawgrass is the site of the Player's Championship of the PGA Tour. In fact, the course is owned by the PGA Tour and located in the same city as its headquarters.

The final two holes are quite memorable and a favorite among tournament fans. The 132-yard, par-3 17th may be the shortest, most intimidating hole around. The route to the green is entirely over water and the green itself is set on a man-made island. The feeling on this tee is not comfortable. The home hole is a 440-yard par-4 shepherded by water all along the left side. The hole turns left so a tee shot placed too far right to avoid the hazard sets up an extremely long approach.

Shadow Creek Golf Club
Address: North Las Vegas, Nevada
Architects: Tom Fazio and Steve Wynn
Established: 1990

The mystery surrounding Shadow Creek has dissipated somewhat since owner Mirage Resorts recently opened to the public albeit on a limited basis. Guests at Shadow Creek may only arrive by limousine from one of Steve Wynn's Las Vegas casinos for a considerably more than nominal fee.

The most amazing thing about Shadow Creek is its oasis-like environment in the middle of the harsh and desolate Southern Nevada desertscape. The property seems to rise from the scrub with thousands of replanted mature Carolina

Pines, an array of rare flowers, exquisitely manicured turf and imported exotic birds to reveal what many feel is one of the top courses in the country.

The design is a classic Tom Fazio layout featuring generally wide fairways, reasonably paced distances and receptive, multi-level greens. The good golfer will score well here and the average golfer will not inflate his handicap too severely. The many turns of Fazio's fairways favor a shotmaker.

Shadow Creek reveals to the public golfer the very best of an exclusive country club environment. The golfer pays dearly to play the course ($1000 including room and transportation) but the reward is a fabulous course and superior service.

PGA West TPC Stadium

Address: La Quinta, California • Architect: Pete Dye
Established: 1986

True to form, perhaps even a bit beyond form, Pete Dye has created a golf course in Southern California that defines the word challenging. PGA West Stadium at one time carried a USGA rating of more than 77. That means a scratch player would be expected to shoot five strokes over par. This is a tough golf course. Lakes come into play on nine holes. Dye has incorporated deep bunkers in inconvenient locations. It is difficult to find a level lie and wayward shots are not treated kindly. The "A" game is required to manage.

A particularly trying hole is the 255-yard, par-3 6th hole appropriately dubbed "Amen." The carry is entirely over a lake that winds around behind the back right portion of the green. The green is relatively deep but it needs to be to hold shots hit with the driver. The dogleg-right 9th hole enjoys water all along the right side. The length of this par-4 is formidable at 450 yards. Bunkers surround the multi-level green. A four here should be considered birdie.

There is a bunker located greenside on the 571-yard, par-5 16th that sits 18 feet below the putting surface. It is so deep that Dye has built in stairs to help the golfer get out. This course is ideal for the golfer looking to test his game.

Sand Hills Golf Club

Address: Mullen, Nebraska
Architects: Bill Coore and Ben Crenshaw
Established: 1995

This extremely private facility caused quite a splash among the golf literati when it opened a few years ago topping nearly every rating list. Ex-PGA Tour superstar Ben Crenshaw has taken his considerable course knowledge into the design arena in fine fashion at Sand Hills.

The links-style soon-to-be classic incorporates notable elevation changes—a feature not normally found on courses built in this notably flat state. Sand Hills is not severely penalizing, especially for the good golfer, lacking in any sort of out-of-bounds. Coore and Crenshaw chose not to include any water hazards or place a tree anywhere that a golf ball might find it. The idea, like Augusta National, was to construct an extremely beautiful track that the well-heeled members would enjoy playing on a regular basis. They succeeded.

Trouble does exist, however, in the form of sand traps that dot the course in ominous locations. The main challenge takes place on the varying greens that are built with large undulations and normally are kept extremely quick. They are of the type that Crenshaw, with his uncanny putting touch, would have excelled at on Tour.

The RULES

The RULES

Golf is a game where integrity is valued above all and fairness is omnipresent. Golf rules exist to help players to remain true to the game, true to their opponents and true to themselves. They do not exist as they do in most other sports to ensure competitors don't cheat. There is an important distinction there. It is utterly common to hear of a golfer competing in a major championship that has called a rules violation on himself, even though no one else could possibly have seen it. The penalty for the infraction may have caused him to lose the tournament or cost him thousands of dollars in potential prize money.

Imagine the shock of hometown fans if a National Basketball Association player ever asked an official to stop the game because he had committed a traveling violation that was not called. Suppose a European footballer requested a free kick for his opponent because he had unintentionally tripped him out of sight of the referee. Team supporters would be beside themselves. In many, indeed most, professional sports, it is considered an advantage to get away with breaking a rule especially if the violator benefits from it. Golf is pleasantly different.

Lest you think all golfers are saints, there are plenty of situations of rules violations on the various world tours either intentional or not. But most infractions tend to occur out of ignorance of a particular rule or an interpretation of that rule. Penalties for breaking the Rules of Golf, whether the intent exists or not, can be very severe depending on the game and the rule broken. The most heinous violation is imposed upon the competitor who unwittingly signs a scorecard that is incorrect—it could have been added improperly, or he or she could have been called for a violation that wasn't discovered until after the scorecards are turned in. Regardless of the reason, a signature applied to an incorrect scorecard calls for the immediate disqualification of the competitor.

Governing Bodies

The Royal & Ancient Golf Club of St. Andrews, Scotland is the keeper of the Rules of Golf for the entire world except for the United States and to a certain extent Canada. The United States Golf Association is home to the Rules for America. These two governing bodies, after decades of agreeing on this and not agreeing on that, have, as of January 2000, adopted the exact same rules and all appendices. Truthfully, most rules have been uniform between the two organizations since a jointly held conference that deemed them so in 1951.

Golf rules exist to help players to remain true to the game, true to their opponents and true to themselves.

To obtain a copy of the Rules of Golf—an extremely wise endeavor for any dedicated golfer—contact:

Royal & Ancient Golf Club
St. Andrews
Fife
KY16 9JD
Scotland

The United States Golf
Association
P.O. Box 708
Far Hills, NJ 07931

The following pages include photographic illustration and text covering the 34 Rules of Golf. While golfers will glean a broad understanding of the Rules from reading this section, the R&A and USGA go much further into specific decisions and interpretations on their respective websites
http://www.randa.org
http://www.usga.org
Readers are encouraged to visit these sites. Two important sections regarding the Rules that are not included in the standard 34 appear in the following pages.

ETIQUETTE
Courtesy on the Course

Safety
Prior to playing a stroke or making a practice swing, the player should ensure that no one is standing close by or in a position to be hit by the club, the ball or any stones, pebbles, twigs or the like which may be moved by the stroke or swing.

Consideration for Other Players
The player who has the honor should be allowed to play before his opponent or fellow-competitor tees his ball. No one should move, talk or stand close to or directly behind the ball or the hole when a player is addressing the ball or making a stroke. No player should play until the players in front are out of range.

Pace of Play
In the interest of all, players should play without delay. Players searching for a ball should signal the players behind them to pass as soon as it becomes apparent that the ball will not easily be found. They should not search for five minutes before doing so. They should not continue play until the players following them have passed and are out of range. When the play of a hole has been completed, players should immediately leave the putting green. If a match fails to keep its place on the course and loses more than one clear hole on the players in front, it should invite the match following to pass.

Priority on the Course
In the absence of special rules, two-ball matches should have precedence over and be entitled to pass any three- or four-ball match, which should invite them through.
A single player has no standing and should give way to a match of any kind. Any match playing a whole round is entitled to pass a match playing a shorter round.

CARE OF THE COURSE

Holes in Bunkers
Before leaving a bunker, a player should carefully fill up and smooth over all holes and footprints made by him.

Replace Divots; Repair Ball-Marks and Damage by Spikes
Through the green, a player should ensure that any turf cut or displaced by him is replaced at once and pressed down and that any damage to the putting green made by a ball is carefully repaired. On completion of the hole by all players in the group, damage to the putting green caused by golf shoe spikes should be repaired.

Damage to Greens—Flagsticks, Bags, etc.
Players should ensure that, when putting down bags or the flagstick, no damage is done to the putting green and that neither they nor their caddies damage the hole by standing close to it, in handling the flagstick or in removing the ball from the hole. The flagstick should be properly replaced in the hole before the players leave the putting green. Players should not damage the putting green by leaning on their putters, particularly when removing the ball from the hole.

Golf Carts
Local notices regulating the movement of golf carts should be strictly observed.

Damage Through Practice Swings
In taking practice swings, players should avoid causing damage to the course, particularly the tees, by removing divots.

DEFINITIONS

Addressing the Ball
A player has "addressed the ball" when he has taken his stance and has also grounded his club, except that in a hazard a player has addressed the ball when he has taken his stance.

Advice
"Advice" is any counsel or suggestion which could influence a player in determining his play, the choice of a club or the method of making a stroke.

Ball in Play
A ball is "in play" as soon as the player has made a stroke on the teeing ground. It remains in play until holed out, except when it is lost, out of bounds or lifted or another ball has been substituted whether or not such substitution is permitted; a ball so substituted becomes the ball in play.

Bunker
A "bunker" is a hazard consisting of a prepared area of ground often a hollow, from which turf or soil has been removed and replaced with sand or the like. Grass-covered ground bordering or within a bunker is not part of the bunker. The margin of a bunker extends vertically downwards, but not upwards. A ball is in a bunker when it lies in or any part of it touches the bunker.

Caddie
A "caddie" is one who carries or handles a player's clubs during play and otherwise assists him accordance with the Rules.
When one caddie is employed by more than one player, he is always deemed to be the caddie of the player whose ball is involved, and equipment carried by him is deemed to be that player's equipment, except when the caddie acts upon specific directions of another player, in which case he is considered to be that other player's caddie.

Casual Water
"Casual water" is any temporary accumulation of water on the course which is visible before or after the player takes his stance and is not in a water hazard.

Snow and natural ice, other than frost, are either casual water or loose impediments, at the option of the player. Manufactured ice is an obstruction. Dew and frost are not casual water. A ball is in casual water when it lies in or any part of it touches the casual water.

Committee
The "Committee" is the committee in charge of the competition or, if the matter does not arise in a competition, the committee in charge of the course.

Competitor
A "competitor" is a player in a stroke competition. A "fellow competitor" is any person with whom the competitor plays. Neither is partner of the other. In stroke play foursome and four-ball competitions, where the context so admits, the word "competitor" or "fellow-competitor" includes his partner.

Course
The "course" is the whole area within which play is permitted (see Rule 33–2).

Equipment
"Equipment" is anything used, worn or carried by or for the player except any ball he has played at the hole being played and any small object, such as a coin or a tee, when used to mark the position of a ball or the extent of an area in which a ball is to be dropped. Equipment includes a golf cart, whether or not motorized. If such a cart is shared by two or more players, the cart and everything in it are deemed to be the equipment of the player whose ball is involved except that, when the cart is being moved by one of the players sharing it, the cart and everything in it are deemed to be that player's equipment.

Note: A ball played at the hole being played is equipment when it has been lifted and not put back into play.

Flagstick
The "flagstick" is a movable straight indicator, with or without bunting or other material attached, centered in the hole to show its position. It shall be circular in cross-section.

Forecaddie
A "forecaddie" is one who is employed by the Committee to indicate to players the position of balls during play. He is an outside agency.

Ground Under Repair
"Ground under repair" is any portion of the course so marked by order of the Committee or so declared by its authorized representative. It includes material piled for removal and a hole made by a greenkeeper, even if not so marked. Stakes and lines defining ground under repair are in such ground. Stakes defining ground under repair are obstructions. The margin of ground under repair extends vertically downwards, but not upwards. A ball is in ground under repair when it lies in or any part of it touches the ground under repair.

Note 1: Grass cuttings and other material left on the course which have been abandoned and are not intended to be removed are not ground under repair unless so marked.

Note 2: The Committee may make a Local Rule prohibiting play from ground under repair or an environmentally-sensitive area which has been defined as ground under repair.

Hazards
A "hazard" is any bunker or water hazard.

Hole
The "hole" shall be 4 inches (108mm) in diameter and at least 4 inches (100mm) deep. If a lining is used, it shall be sunk at least one inch (25 mm) below the putting green surface unless the nature of the soil makes it impracticable to do

so; its outer diameter shall not exceed 4 inches (108mm).

Holed

A ball is "holed" when it is at rest within the circumference of the hole and all of it is below the level of the lip of the hole.

Honor

The side entitled to play first from the teeing ground is said to have the "honor."

Lateral Water Hazard

A "lateral water hazard" is a water hazard or that part of a water hazard so situated that it is not possible or is deemed by the Committee to be impracticable to drop a ball behind the water hazard in accordance with Rule 26–1b.

That part of a water hazard to be played as a lateral water hazard should be distinctively marked. A ball is in a lateral water hazard when it lies in or any part of it touches the lateral water hazard.

Note 1: Lateral water hazards should be defined by red stakes or lines.

Note 2: The Committee may make a Local Rule prohibiting play from an environmentally-sensitive area which has been defined as a lateral water hazard.

Line of Play

The "line of play" is the direction which the player wishes his ball to take after a stroke, plus a reasonable distance on either side of the intended direction. The line of play extends vertically upwards from the ground, but does not extend beyond the hole.

Line of Putt

The "line of putt" is the line which the player wishes his ball to take after a stroke on the putting green. Except with respect to Rule 16–1e, the line of putt includes a reasonable distance on either side of the intended line. The line of putt does not extend beyond the hole.

Loose Impediments

"Loose impediments" are natural objects such as stones, leaves, twigs, branches and the like, dung, worms and insects and casts or heaps made by them, provided they are not fixed or growing, are not solidly embedded and do not adhere to the ball.

Sand and loose soil are loose impediments on the putting green, but not elsewhere.

Snow and natural ice, other than frost, are either casual water or loose impediments, at the option of the player. Manufactured ice is an obstruction. Dew and frost are not loose impediments.

Lost Ball

A ball is "lost" if:
a. It is not found or identified as his by the player within five minutes after the player's side or his or their caddies have begun to search for it; or
b. The player has put another ball into play under the Rules, even though he may not have searched for the original ball; or
c. The player has played any stroke with a provision ball from the place where the original ball is likely to be or from a point nearer the hole than that place, whereupon the provisional ball becomes the ball in play.

Time spent in playing a wrong ball is not counted in the five-minute period allowed for search.

Marker

A "marker" is one who is appointed by the Committee to record a competitor's score in stroke play. He may be a fellow-competitor. He is not a referee.

Move or Moved

A ball is deemed to have "moved" if it leaves its position and comes to rest in any other place.

Observer

An "observer" is one who is appointed by the Committee to assist a referee to decide questions of fact and to report to him any breach of a Rule. An observer should not attend the flagstick, stand or mark the position of the hole, or lift the ball or mark its position.

Obstructions

An "obstruction" is anything artificial, including the artificial surfaces and sides of roads and paths and manufactured ice, except:
a. Objects defining out of bounds, such as walls, fences, stakes and railings;
b. Any part of an immovable artificial object which is out of bounds; and
c. Any construction declared by the Committee to be an integral part of the course.

Out of Bounds

"Out of bounds" is ground on which play is prohibited.

When out of bounds is defined by reference to stakes or a fence or as being beyond stakes or a fence, the out of bounds line is determined by the nearest inside points of the stakes or fence posts at ground level excluding angled support.

When out of bounds is defined by a line on the ground, the line itself is out of bounds.

The out of bounds line extends vertically upwards and downwards. A ball is out of bounds when all of it lies out of bounds.

A player may stand out of bounds to play a ball lying within bounds.

Outside Agency

An "outside agency" is any agency not part of the match or, in stroke play, not part of the competitor's side, and includes a referee, a marker, an observer and a forecaddie. Neither wind nor water is an outside agency.

Partner

A "partner" is a player associated with another player on the same side. In a threesome, foursome, best-ball or four-ball match, where the context so admits, the word "player" includes his partner or partners.

Penalty Stroke

A "penalty stroke" is one added to the score of a player or side under certain Rules. In a threesome or foursome, penalty strokes do not affect the order of play.

Provisional Ball
A "provisional ball" is a ball played under Rule 27-2 for a ball which may be lost outside a water hazard or may be out of bounds.

Putting Green
The "putting green" is all ground of the hole being played which is specially prepared for putting or otherwise defined as such by the Committee. A ball is on the putting green when any part of it touches the putting green.

Referee
A "referee" is one who is appointed by the Committee to accompany players to decide questions of fact and apply the Rules. He shall act on any breach of a Rule which he observes or is reported to him.

A referee should not attend the flagstick, stand at or mark the position of the hole, or lift the ball or mark its position.

Rub of the Green
A "rub of the green" occurs when a ball in motion is accidentally deflected or stopped by any outside agency (see Rule 19–1).

Rule
The term "Rule" includes Local Rules made by the Committee under Rule 33–8a.

Sides and Matches
Side: A player, or two or more players who are partners.
Single: A match in which one plays against another.
Threesome: A match in which one plays against two, and each side plays one ball.
Foursome: A match in which two play against two, and each side plays one ball.
Three-Ball: A match play competition in which three play against one another, each playing his own ball. Each player is playing two distinct matches.
Best-Ball: A match in which one plays against the better ball of two or the best ball of three players.
Four-Ball: A match in which two play their better ball against the better ball of two other players.

Stance
Taking the "stance" consists in a player placing his feet in position for and preparatory to making a stroke.

Stipulated Round
The "stipulated round" consists of playing the holes of the course in their correct sequence unless otherwise authorized by the Committee.

The number of holes in a stipulated round is 18 unless a small number is authorized by the Committee. As to extension of stipulated round in match play, see Rule 2–3.

Stroke
A "stroke" is the forward movement of the club made with the intention of fairly striking at and moving the ball, but if a player checks his downswing voluntarily before the clubhead reaches the ball he is deemed not to have made a stroke.

Teeing Ground
The "teeing ground" is the start place for the hole to be played. It is a rectangular area two club-lengths in depth, the front and the sides of which are defined by the outside limits of two tee-markers. A ball is outside the teeing ground when all of it lies outside the teeing ground.

Through the Green
"Through the green" is the whole area of the course except:
a. The teeing ground and putting green of the hole being played; and
b. All hazards on the course.

Water Hazard
A "water hazard" is any sea, lake, pond, river, ditch, surface drainage ditch or other open water course (whether or not containing water) and anything of a similar nature. All ground or water within the margin of a water hazard is part of the water hazard. The margin of a water hazard extends vertically upwards and downwards. Stakes and the lines defining the margins of water hazards are in the hazards. Such stakes are obstructions. A ball is in a water hazard when it lies in or any part of it touches the water hazard.

Note 1: Water hazards (other than lateral water hazards) should be defined by yellow stakes or lines.

Note 2: The Committee may make a Local Rule prohibiting play from an environmentally-sensitive area which has been defined as a water hazard.

Wrong Ball
A "wrong ball" is any ball other than the player's: a. Ball in play, b. Provisional ball, or c. Second ball played under Rule 3–3 or Rule 20–7b in stroke play.

Note: Ball in play includes a ball substituted for the ball in play whether or not such substitution is permitted.

The GAME

RULE 1. THE GAME

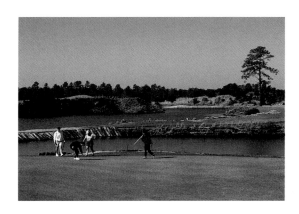

1–1. General

The Game of Golf consists in playing a ball from the teeing ground into the hole by a stroke or successive strokes in accordance with the Rules.

1–2. Exerting Influence on Ball

No player or caddie shall take any action to influence the position or the movement of a ball except in accordance with the Rules.
Penalty for Breach of Rule 1–2: Match play—Loss of hole;
Stroke play—Two strokes.

Note: In the case of a serious breach of Rule 1–2, the Committee may impose a penalty of disqualification.

1–3. Agreement to Waive Rules

Players shall not agree to exclude the operation of any Rule or to waive any penalty incurred.

Penalty for Breach of Rule 1–3: Match play—Disqualification of both sides; Stroke play—Disqualification of competitors concerned.
(Agreeing to play out of turn in stroke play—Rule 10–2c.)

1–4. Points Not Covered by Rules

If any point in dispute is not covered by the Rules, the decision shall be made in accordance with equity.

RULE 2. MATCH PLAY

2–1. Winner of Hole; Reckoning of Holes

In match play the game is played by holes.

Except as otherwise provided in the Rules, a hole is won by the side which holes its ball in the fewer strokes. In a handicap match the lower net score wins the hole.

The reckoning of holes is kept by the terms: so many "holes up" or "all square," and so many "to play." A side is "dormie" when it is as many holes up as there are holes remaining to be played.

2–2. Halved Hole

A hole is halved if each side holes out in the same number of strokes.

When a player has holed out and his opponent has been left with a stroke for the half, if the player thereafter incurs a penalty, the hole is halved.

2–3. Winner of Match

A match (which consists of a stipulated round, unless otherwise decreed by the Committee) is won by the side which is leading by a number of holes greater than the number of holes remaining to be played.

The Committee may, for the purpose of settling a tie, extend the stipulated round to as many holes as are required for a match to be won.

2–4. Concession of Next Stroke, Hole or Match

When the opponent's ball is at rest or is deemed to be at rest under Rule 16–2, the player may concede the opponent to have holed out with his next stroke and the ball may be removed by either side with a club or otherwise.

A player may concede a hole or a match at any time prior to the conclusion of the hole or the match.

Concession of a stroke, hole or match may not be declined or withdrawn.

2–5. Claims

In match play, if a doubt or dispute arises between the players and duly authorized representative of the Committee is available within a reasonable time, the players shall continue the match without delay.

Any claim, if it is to be considered by the Committee, must be made before any player in the match plays from the next teeing ground or, in the case of the last hole of the match, before all players in the match leave the putting green.

No later claim shall be considered unless it is based on facts previously unknown to the player making the claim and the player making the claim had been given wrong information (Rules 6–2a and 9) by an opponent. In any case, no later claim shall be considered after the result of the match has been officially announced, unless the Committee is satisfied that the opponent knew he was giving wrong information.

2–6. General Penalty

The penalty for a breach of a Rule in match play is loss of hole except when otherwise provided.

RULE 3. STROKE PLAY

3–1. Winner

The competitor who plays the stipulated round or rounds in the fewest strokes is the winner.

3–2. Failure to Hole Out
If a competitor fails to hole out at any hole and does not correct his mistake before he plays a stroke from the next teeing ground or, in the case of the last hole of the round, before he leaves the putting green, he shall be disqualified.

3–3. Doubt as to Procedure
a. Procedure

In stroke play only, when during play of a hole a competitor is doubtful of his rights or procedure, he may, without penalty, play a second ball. After the situation which caused the doubt has arisen, the competitor should, before taking further action, announce to his marker or a fellow-competitor his decision to invokee this Rule and the ball with which he will score if the Rules permit.

The competitor shall report the facts to the Committee before returning his score card unless he scores the same with both balls; if he fails to do so, he shall be disqualified.

b. Determination of Score for Hole

If the Rules allow the procedure selected in advance by the competitor, the score with the ball selected shall be his score for the hole.

If the competitor fails to announce in advance his decision to invoke this Rule or his selection, the score with the original ball or, if the original ball is not one of the balls being played, the first ball put into play shall count if the Rules allow the procedure adopted for such ball.

Note: A second ball played under Rule 3-3 is not a provisional ball under Rule 27–2.

3–4. Refusal to Comply with a Rule

If a competitor refuses to comply with a Rule affecting the rights of another competitor, he shall be disqualified.

3–5. General Penalty

The penalty for a breach of a Rule in stroke play is two strokes except when otherwise provided.

RULE 4. CLUBS

4–1. Form and Make of Clubs

A club is an implement designed to be used for striking the ball.
A putter is a club with a loft not exceeding ten degrees
designed primarily for use on the putting green.

The player's clubs shall conform with the provisions of this Rule
and with the specifications and interpretations set forth in Appendix II.

a. General

The club shall be composed of a shaft and a head.
All parts of the club shall be fixed so that the club is one unit. The club shall not be
designed to be adjustable except for weight (see also Appendix II).
The club shall not be substantially different from the traditional and customary form and
make, and shall have no external attachments except as otherwise permitted by the Rules.

b. Shaft

The shaft shall be straight, with the same
bending and twisting properties in any direction,
and shall be attached to the clubhead at the heel
either directly or through a single plain neck and/
or socket. A putter shaft may be attached to any
point in the head.

c. Grip

The grip consists of that part of the shaft designed
to be held by the player and any material added
to it for the purpose of obtaining a firm hold.
The grip shall be straight and plain in form,
shall extend to the end of the shaft and
shall not be molded for any part of the hands.

d. Clubhead

The distance from the heel to the toe of the clubhead shall be greater than the distance from the face to the back. The clubhead shall be generally plain in shape. The clubhead shall have only one striking face, except that a putter may have two such faces if their characteristics are the same, and they are opposite each other.

e. Club Face

The face of the club shall be hard and rigid (some exceptions may be made for putters) and, except for such markings as are permitted by Appendix II, shall be smooth and shall not have any degree of concavity.

f. Wear and Alteration

A club which conforms with Rule 4–1 when new is deemed to conform after wear through normal use. Any part of a club which has been purposely altered is regarded as new and must conform, in the altered state, with the Rules.

g. Damage

If a player's club ceases to conform with Rule 4–1 because of damage sustained in the normal course of play, the player may:
(i) use the club in its damaged state, but only for the remainder of the stipulated round during which such damage was sustained; or
(ii) without unduly delaying play, repair it.
A club which ceases to conform because of damage sustained other than in the normal course of play shall not subsequently be used during the round.
(Damage changing playing characteristics of club—see Rule 4–2.)
(Damage rendering club unfit for play—see Rule 4–4a.)

4–2. Playing Characteristics Changed

During a stipulated round, the playing characteristics of a club shall not be purposely changed by adjustment or by any other means.

If the playing characteristics of a player's club are changed during a round because of damage sustained in the normal course of play, the player may:
(i) use the club in its altered state; or
(ii) without unduly delaying play, repair it.

If the playing characteristics of a player's club are changed because of damage sustained other than in the normal course of play, the club shall not subsequently be used during the round.

Damage to a club which occurred prior to a round may be repaired during the round, provided the playing characteristics are not changed and play is not unduly delayed.

4–3. Foreign Material

Foreign material must not be applied to the club face for the purpose of influencing the movement of the ball.
Penalty for Breach of Rule 4–1, –2 or –3:
Disqualification.

4–4. Maximum of Fourteen Clubs

a. Selection and Replacement of Clubs

The player shall start a stipulated round with not more than fourteen clubs. He is limited to the clubs thus selected for that round except that, without unduly delaying play, he may:

(i) if he started with fewer than fourteen clubs, add any number provided his total number does not exceed fourteen; and

(ii) replace, with any club, a club which becomes unfit for play in the normal course of play.

The addition or replacement of a club or clubs may not be made by borrowing any club selected for play by any other person playing on the course.

b. Partners May Share Clubs

Partners may share clubs, provided that the total number of clubs carried by the partners so sharing does not exceed fourteen.

Penalty for Breach of Rule 4–4a or b, Regardless of Number of Excess Clubs Carried:

Match play—At the conclusion of the hole at which the breach is discovered, the state of the match shall be adjusted by deducting one hole for each hole at which a breach occurred.

Maximum deduction per round: two holes.

Stroke play—Two strokes for each hole at which any breach occurred;

maximum penalty per round: four strokes.

Bogey and par competitions—Penalties as in match play.

Stableford competitions—see Note to Rule 32–1b.

c. Excess Club Declared Out of Play

Any club carried or used in breach of this Rule shall be declared out of play by the player immediately upon discovery that a breach has occurred and thereafter shall not be used by the player during the round.

Penalty for Breach of Rule 4–4c: Disqualification.

RULE 5. THE BALL

5–1. General

The ball the player uses shall conform to requirements specified in Appendix III on maximum weight, minimum size, spherical symmetry, initial velocity and overall distance.

Note: The Committee may require, in the conditions of a competition (Rule 33–1), that the ball the player uses must be named on the current List of Conforming Golf Balls issued by the United States Golf Association.

5–2. Foreign Material

Foreign material must not be applied to a ball for the purpose of changing its playing characteristics.

Penalty for Breach of Rule 5–1 or 5–2: Disqualification.

5–3. Ball Unfit for Play

A ball is unfit for play if it is visibly cut, cracked or out of shape.

A ball is not unfit for play solely because mud or other materials adhere to it, its surface is scratched or scraped or its paint is damaged or discolored.

If a player has reason to believe his ball has become unfit for play during the play of the hole being played, he may during the play of such hole lift his ball without penalty to determine whether it is unfit.

Before lifting the ball, the player must announce his intention to his opponent in match play or his marker or a fellow-competitor in stroke play and mark the position of the ball. He may then lift and examine the ball without cleaning it and must give his opponent, marker or fellow-competitor an opportunity to examine the ball. If he fails to comply with this procedure, he shall incur a penalty of one stroke.

If it is determined that the ball has become unfit for play during play of the hole being played, the player may substitute another ball, placing it on the spot where the original ball lay. Otherwise, the original ball shall be replaced.

If a ball breaks into pieces as a result of a stroke, the stroke shall be cancelled and the player shall play a ball without penalty as nearly as possible at the spot from which the original ball was played (see Rule 20–5).

*Penalty for Breach of Rule 5–3: Match play—Loss of hole; Stroke play—Two strokes.

*If a player incurs the general penalty for breach of Rule 5–3, no additional penalty under the Rule shall be applied.

Note: If the opponent, marker or fellow-competitor wishes to dispute a claim of unfitness, he must do so before the player plays another ball. (Cleaning ball lifted from putting green or under any other Rule—see Rule 21.)

RULE 6. THE PLAYER

A "marker" is one who is appointed by the Committee to record a competitor's score in stroke play. He may be a fellow-competitor. He is not a referee.

6–1. Conditions of Competition

The player is responsible for knowing the conditions under which the competition is to be played (Rule 33–1).

6–2. Handicap
a. Match Play

Before starting a match in a handicap competition, the players should determine from one another their respective handicaps. If a player begins the match having declared a higher handicap which would affect the number of strokes given or received, he shall be disqualified; otherwise, the player shall play off the declared handicap.

b. Stroke Play

In any round of a handicap competition, the competitor shall ensure that his handicap is recorded on his score card before it is returned to the Committee. If no handicap is recorded on his score card before it is returned, or if the recorded handicap is higher than that to which he is entitled and this affects the number of strokes received, he shall be disqualified from that round of the handicap competition; otherwise, the score shall stand.

Note: It is the player's responsibility to know the holes at which handicap strokes are to be given or received.

6–3. Time of Starting and Groups
a. Time of Starting

The player shall start at the time laid down by the Committee.

b. Groups

In stroke play, the competitor shall remain throughout the round in the group arranged by the Committee unless the Committee authorizes or ratifies a change.

Penalty for Breach of Rule 6–3: Disqualification.

(Best-ball and four-ball play—see Rules 30–3a and 31–2.)

Note: The Committee may provide in the conditions of a competition (Rule 33–1) that, if the player arrives at his starting point, ready to play, within five minutes after his starting time, in the absence of circumstances which warrant waiving the penalty of disqualification as provided in Rule 33–7, the penalty for failure to start on time is loss of the first hole in match play or two strokes at the first hole in stroke play instead of disqualification.

6–4. Caddie

The player may have only one caddie at any one time, under penalty of disqualification. For any breach of a Rule by his caddie, the player incurs the applicable penalty.

6–5. Ball

The responsibility for playing the proper ball rests with the player. Each player should put an identification mark on his ball.

6–6. Scoring in Stroke Play

a. Recording Scores

After each hole the marker should check the score with the competitor and record it. On completion of the round the marker shall sign the card and hand it to the competitor. If more than one marker records the scores, each shall sign for the part for which he is responsible.

b. Signing and Returning Card

After completion of the round, the competitor should check his score for each hole and settle any doubtful points with the Committee. He shall ensure that the marker has signed the card, countersign the card himself and return it to the Committee as soon as possible.

Penalty for Breach of Rule 6–6b: Disqualification.

c. Alteration of Card

No alteration may be made on a card after the competitor has returned it to the Committee.

d. Wrong Score for Hole

The competitor is responsible for the correctness of the score recorded for each hole on his card. If he returns a score for any hole lower than actually taken, he shall be disqualified. If he returns a score for any hole higher than actually taken, the score as returned shall stand.

Note 1: The Committee is responsible for the addition of scores and application of the handicap recorded on the card—see Rule 33–5.

Note 2: In four-ball stroke play, see also Rule 31–4 and –7a.

6–7. Undue Delay; Slow Play

The player shall play without undue delay and in accordance with any pace of play guidelines which may be laid down by the Committee. Between completion of a hole and playing from the next teeing ground, the player shall not unduly delay play.

Penalty for Breach of Rule 6–7: Match play—Loss of hole; Stroke play—Two strokes.

For subsequent offense—Disqualification.

Note 1: If the player unduly delays play between holes, he is delaying the play of the next hole and the penalty applies to that hole.

Note 2: For the purpose of preventing slow play, the Committee may, in the conditions of a competition (Rule 33–1), lay down pace of play guidelines including maximum periods of time allowed to complete a stipulated round, a hole or a stroke.

In stroke play only, the Committee may, in such a condition, modify the penalty for a breach of this Rule as follows: First offense—One stroke; Second offense—Two strokes. For subsequent offense—Disqualification.

6–8. Discontinuance of Play

a. When Permitted

The player shall not discontinue play unless:

(i) the Committee has suspended play;

(ii) he believes there is danger from lightning;

(iii) he is seeking a decision from the Committee on a doubtful or disputed point (see Rules 2–5 and 34–3); or

(iv) there is some other good reason such as sudden illness.

Bad weather is not of itself a good reason for discontinuing play.

If the player discontinues play without specific permission from the Committee, he shall report to the Committee as soon as practicable. If he does so and the Committee considers his reason satisfactory, the player incurs no penalty. Otherwise, the player shall be disqualified.

Exception in match play: Players discontinuing match play by agreement are not subject to disqualification unless by so doing the competition is delayed.

Note: Leaving the course does not of itself constitute discontinuance of play.

b. Procedure when Play Suspended by Committee

When play is suspended by the Committee, if the players in a match or group are between the play of two holes, they shall not resume play until the Committee has ordered a resumption of play. If they are in the process of playing a hole, they may continue provided they do so without delay. If they choose to continue, they shall discontinue either before or immediately after completing the hole, and shall not thereafter resume play until the Committee has ordered a resumption of play.

When play has been suspended by the Committee, the player shall resume play when the Committee has ordered a resumption of play.

Penalty for Breach of Rule 6–8b: Disqualification.

Note: The Committee may provide in the conditions of a competition (Rule 33–1) that, in potentially dangerous situations, play shall be discontinued immediately following a suspension of play by the Committee. If a player fails to discontinue play immediately, he shall be disqualified unless circumstances warrant waiving such penalty as provided in Rule 33–7. (Resumption of play—see Rule 33–2d.)

c. Lifting Ball When Play Discontinued

When during the play of a hole a player discontinues play under Rule 6–8a, he may lift his ball. A ball may be cleaned when so lifted. If a ball has been so lifted, the player shall, when play is resumed, place a ball on the spot from which the original ball was lifted.

Penalty for Breach of Rule 6–8c: Match play—Loss of hole; Stroke play—Two strokes.

RULE 7. PRACTICE

7–1. Before or Between Rounds

a. Match Play

On any day of a match play competition, a player may practice on the competition course before a round.

b. Stroke Play

On any day of a stroke competition or play-off, a competitor shall not practice on the competition course or test the surface of any putting green on the course before a round or play-off. When two or more rounds of a stroke competition are to be played over consecutive days, practice between those rounds on any competition course remaining to be played is prohibited.

Exception: Practice putting or chipping on or near the first teeing ground before starting a round or play-off is permitted.

Penalty for Breach of Rule 7–1b: Disqualification.

Note: The Committee may in the conditions of a competition (Rule 33–1) prohibit practice on the competition course on any day of a match play competition or permit practice on the competition course or part of the course (Rule 33–2c) on any day of or between rounds of a stroke competition.

7–2. During Round

A player shall not play a practice stroke either during the play of a hole or between the play of two holes except that, between the play of two holes, the player may practice putting or chipping on or near the putting green of the hole last played, any practice putting green or the teeing ground of the next hole to be played in the round, provided such practice stroke is not played from a hazard and does not unduly delay play (Rule 6–7).

Strokes played in continuing the play of a hole, the result of which has been decided, are not practice strokes.

Exception: When play has been suspended by the Committee, a player may, prior to resumption of play, practice (a) as provided in this Rule, (b) anywhere other than on the competition course and (c) as otherwise permitted by the Committee.

Penalty for Breach of Rule 7–2: Match play—Loss of hole; Stroke play—Two strokes. In the event of a breach between the play of two holes, the penalty applies to the next hole.

Note 1: A practice swing is not a practice stroke and may be taken at any place, provided the player does not breach the Rules.

Note 2: The Committee may prohibit practice on or near the putting green of the hole last played.

RULE 8. ADVICE;
INDICATING LINE OF PLAY

"Advice" is any counsel or suggestion which could influence a player in determining his play, the choice of a club or the method of making a stroke. Information on the Rules or on matters of public information, such as the position of hazards or the flagstick on the putting green, is not advice. The "line of play" is the direction which the player wishes his ball to take after a stroke, plus a reasonable distance on either side of the intended direction. The line of play extends vertically upwards from the ground, but does not extend beyond the hole.

8–1. Advice

During a stipulated round, a player shall not give advice to anyone in the competition except his partner.
A player may ask for advice during a stipulated round from only his partner or either of their caddies.

8–2. Indicating Line of Play

a. Other Than On Putting Green

Except on the putting green, a player may have the line of play indicated to him by anyone, but no one shall be positioned by the player on or close to the line or an extension of the line beyond the hole while the stroke is being played. Any mark placed during the play of a hole by the player or with his knowledge to indicate the line shall be removed before the stroke is played.

Exception: Flagstick attended or held up—see Rule 17–1.

b. On the Putting Green

When the player's ball is on the putting green, the player, his partner or either of their caddies may, before but not during the stroke, point out a line for putting, but in so doing the putting green shall not be touched. No mark shall be placed anywhere to indicate a line for putting.

Penalty for Breach of Rule: Match play—Loss of hole; Stroke play—Two strokes.

Note: The Committee may, in the conditions of a team competition (Rule 33–1), permit each team to appoint one person who may give advice (including pointing out a linefor putting) to members of that team. The Committee may lay down conditions relating to the appointment and permitted conduct of such person, who must be identified to the Committee before giving advice.

RULE 9. INFORMATION
AS TO STROKES TAKEN

9–1. General

The number of strokes a player has taken shall include any penalty strokes incurred.

A player who has incurred a penalty shall inform his opponent as soon as practicable, unless he is obviously proceeding under a Rule involving a penalty and this has been observed by his opponent. If he fails so to inform his opponent, he shall be deemed to have given wrong information, even if he was not aware that he had incurred a penalty. An opponent is entitled to ascertain from the player, during the play of a hole, the number of strokes he has taken and, after play of a hole, the number of strokes taken on the hole just completed.

If during the play of a hole the player gives or is deemed to give wrong information as to the number of strokes taken, he shall incur no penalty if he corrects the mistake before his opponent has played his next stroke. If the player fails so to correct the wrong information, he shall lose the hole.

If after play of a hole the player gives or is deemed to give wrong information as to the number of strokes taken on the hole just completed and this affects the opponent's understanding of the result of the hole, he shall incur no penalty if he corrects his mistake before any player plays from the next teeing ground or, in the case of the last hole of the match, before all players leave the putting green. If the player fails so to correct the wrong information, he shall lose the hole.

9–3. Stroke Play

A competitor who has incurred a penalty should inform his marker as soon as practicable.

RULE 10. ORDER OF PLAY

10-1. Match Play

a. Teeing Ground

The side entitled to play first from the teeing ground is said to have the "honor." The side which shall have the honor at the first teeing ground shall be determined by the order of the draw. In the absence of a draw, the honor should be decided by lot. The side which wins a hole shall take the honor at the next tee. If a hole has been halved, the side which had the honor at the previous teeing ground shall retain it.

b. Other Than on Teeing Ground

When the balls are in play, the ball farther from the hole shall be played first. If the balls are equidistant from the hole, the ball to be played first should be decided by lot.

Exception: Rule 30–3c (best-ball and four-ball match play).

c. Playing Out of Turn

If a player plays when his opponent should have played, the opponent may immediately require the player to cancel the stroke so played and, in correct order, play a ball without penalty as nearly as possible at the spot from which the original ball was last played (see Rule 20–5).

10–2. Stroke Play

a. Teeing Ground

The competitor entitled to play first from the teeing ground is said to have the "honor." The competitor who shall have the honor at the first teeing ground shall be determined by the order of the draw. In the absence of a draw, the honor should be decided by lot. The competitor with the lowest score at a hole shall take the honor at the next teeing ground. The competitor with the second lowest score shall play next and so on. If two or more competitors have the same score at a hole, they shall play from the next teeing ground in the same order as at the previous teeing ground.

b. Other Than on Teeing Ground

When the balls are in play, the ball farthest from the hole shall be played first. If two or more balls are equidistant from the hole, the ball to be played first should be decided by lot.
Exceptions: Rules 22 (ball interfering with or assisting play) and 31–5 (four-ball stroke play).

c. Playing Out of Turn

If a competitor plays out of turn, no penalty is incurred and the ball shall be played as it lies. If, however, the Committee determines that competitors have agreed to play in an order other than that set forth in Clauses 2a and 2b of this Rule to give one of them an advantage, they shall be disqualified. (Incorrect order of play in threesomes and foursomes stroke play—see Rule 29–3.)

10–3. Provisional Ball or Second Ball from Teeing Ground

If a player plays a provisional ball or a second ball from a teeing ground, he should do so after his opponent or fellow-competitor has played his first stroke. If a player plays a provisional ball or a second ball out of turn, Clauses 1c and 2c of this Rule shall apply.

10–4. Ball Moved in Measuring

If a ball is moved in measuring to determine which ball is farther from the hole, no penalty is incurred and the ball shall be replaced.

RULE 11. TEEING GROUND

The "teeing ground" is the starting place for the hole to be played. It is a rectangular area two club-lengths in depth, the front and the sides of which are defined by the outside limits of two tee-markers. A ball is outside the teeing ground when all of it lies outside the teeing ground.

11–1. Teeing

In teeing, the ball may be placed on the ground, on an irregularity of surface created by the player on the ground or on a tee, sand or other substance in order to raise it off the ground.

A player may stand outside the teeing ground to play a ball within it.

11–2. Tee-Markers

Before a player plays his first stroke with any ball from the teeing ground of the hole being played, the tee-markers are deemed to be fixed. In such circumstances, if the player moves or allows to be moved a tee-marker for the purpose of avoiding interference with his stance, the area of his intended swing or his line of play, he shall incur the penalty for a breach of Rule 13–2.

11–3. Ball Falling Off Tee

If a ball, when not in play, falls off a tee or is knocked off a tee by the player in addressing it, it may be re-teed without penalty, but if a stroke is made at the ball in these circumstances, whether the ball is moving or not, the stroke counts but no penalty is incurred.

11–4. Playing from Outside Teeing Ground

a. Match Play

If a player, when starting a hole, plays a ball from outside the teeing ground, the opponent may immediately require the player to cancel the stroke so played and play a ball from within the teeing ground, without penalty.

b. Stroke Play

If a competitor, when starting a hole, plays a ball from outside the teeing ground, he shall incur a penalty of two strokes and shall then play a ball from within the teeing ground.

If the competitor plays a stroke from the next teeing ground without first correcting his mistake or, in the case of the last hole of the round, leaves the putting green without first declaring his intention to correct his mistake, he shall be disqualified.

Strokes played by a competitor from outside the teeing ground do not count in his score.

11–5. Playing from Wrong Teeing Ground

The provisions of Rule 11–4 apply.

RULE 12. SEARCHING
FOR & IDENTIFYING BALL

A "hazard" is any bunker or water hazard.

A "bunker" is a hazard consisting of a prepared area of ground, often a hollow, from which turf or soil has been removed and replaced with sand or the like. Grass-covered ground bordering or within a bunker is not part of the bunker. The margin of a bunker extends vertically downwards, but not upwards. A ball is in a bunker when it lies in or any part of it touches the bunker.

A "water hazard" is any sea, lake, pond, river, ditch, surface drainage ditch or other open water course (whether or not containing water) and anything of a similar nature.

All ground or water within the margin of a water hazard is part of the water hazard. The margin of a water hazard extends vertically upwards and downwards. Stakes and lines defining the margins of water hazards are in the hazards. Such stakes are obstructions. A ball is in a water hazard when it lies in or any part of it touches the water hazard.

12–1. Searching for Ball; Seeing Ball

In searching for his ball anywhere on the course, the player may touch or bend long grass, rushes, bushes, whins, heather or the like, but only to the extent necessary to find and identify it, provided that this does not improve the lie of the ball, the area of his intended swing or his line of play.

A player is not necessarily entitled to see his ball when playing a stroke.

In a hazard, if a ball is covered by loose impediments or sand, the player may remove by probing, raking or other means as much thereof as will enable him to see a part of the ball. If an excess is removed, no penalty is incurred and the ball shall be re-covered so that only a part of the ball is visible. If the ball is moved in such removal, no penalty is incurred; the ball shall be replaced and, if necessary, re-covered. As to removal of loose impediments outside a hazard, see Rule 23.

If a ball lying in casual water, ground under repair or a hole, cast or runway made by a burrowing animal, a reptile or a bird is accidentally moved during search, no penalty is incurred; the ball shall be replaced, unless the player elects to proceed under Rule 25–1b.

If a ball is believed to be lying in water in a water hazard, the player may probe for it with a club or otherwise. If the ball is moved in so doing, no penalty is incurred; the ball shall be replaced, unless the player elects to proceed under Rule 26–1.

Penalty for Breach of Rule 12–1: Match play—Loss of hole; Stroke play—Two strokes.

12–2. Identifying Ball

The responsibility for playing the proper ball rests with the player. Each player should put an identification mark on his ball.

Except in a hazard, the player may, without penalty, lift a ball he believes to be his own for the purpose of identification and clean it to the extent necessary for identification. If the ball is the player's ball, he shall replace it. Before lifting the ball, the player must announce his intention to his opponent in match play or his marker or a fellow-competitor in stroke play and mark the position of the ball. He must then give his opponent, marker or fellow-competitor an opportunity to observe the lifting and replacement. If he lifts his ball without announcing his intention in advance, marking the position of the ball or giving his opponent, marker or fellow-competitor an opportunity to observe, or if he lifts his ball for identification in a hazard, or cleans it more than necessary for identification, he shall incur a penalty of one stroke and the ball shall be replaced.

If a player who is required to replace a ball fails to do so, he shall incur the penalty for a breach of Rule 20–3a, but no additional penalty under Rule 12–2 shall be applied.

RULE 13. BALL PLAYED
AS IT LIES; AREA OF INTENDED SWING & LINE OF PLAY; STANCE

A "hazard" is any bunker or water hazard.
A "bunker" is a hazard consisting of a prepared area of ground, often a hollow, from which turf or soil has been removed and replaced with sand or the like. Grass-covered ground bordering or within a bunker is not part of the bunker. The margin of a bunker extends vertically downwards, but not upwards. A ball is in a bunker when it lies in or any part of it touches the bunker.
A "water hazard" is any sea, lake, pond, river, ditch, surface drainage ditch or other open water course (whether or not containing water) and anything of a similar nature. All ground or water within the margin of a water hazard is part of the water hazard. The margin of a water hazard extends vertically upwards and downwards. Stakes and lines defining the margins of water hazards are in the hazards. Such stakes are obstructions. A ball is in a water hazard when it lies in or any part of it touches the water hazard.
The "line of play" is the direction which the player wishes his ball to take after a stroke, plus a reasonable distance on either side of the intended direction. The line of play extends vertically upwards from the ground, but does not extend beyond the hole.

13–1. Ball Played as It Lies

The ball shall be played as it lies, except as otherwise provided in the Rules. (Ball at rest moved—see Rule 18.)

13–2. Improving Lie, Area of Intended Swing or Line of Play

Except as provided in the Rules, a player shall not improve or allow to be improved: the position or lie of his ball, the area of his intended swing, his line of play or a reasonable extension of that line beyond the hole or the area in which he is to drop or place a ball by any of the following actions: moving, bending or breaking anything growing or fixed (including immovable obstructions and objects defining out of bounds) or removing or pressing down sand, loose soil, replaced divots, other cut turf placed in position or other irregularities of surface except as follows: as may occur in fairly taking his stance, in making a stroke or the backward movement of his club for a stroke, on the teeing ground in creating or eliminating irregularities of surface, or on the putting green in removing sand and loose soil as provided in Rule 16–1a or in repairing damage as provided in Rule 16–1c. The club may be grounded only lightly and shall not be pressed on the ground.

Exception: Ball in hazard—see Rule 13–4.

RULE 14. STRIKING THE BALL

A "stroke" is the forward movement of the club made with the intention of fairly striking at and moving the ball, but if a player checks his downswing voluntarily before the clubhead reaches the ball he is deemed not to have made a stroke.

14–1. Ball to Be Fairly Struck At

The ball shall be fairly struck at with the head of the club and must not be pushed, scraped or spooned.

14–2. Assistance

In making a stroke, a player shall not accept physical assistance or protection from the elements.
Penalty for Breach of Rule 14–1or –2: Match play—Loss of hole; Stroke play—Two strokes.

14–3. Artificial Devices and Unusual Equipment

A player in doubt as to whether use of an item would constitute a breach of Rule 14–3 should consult the United States Golf Association.

A manufacturer may suit to the United States Golf Association a sample of an item which is to be manufactured for a ruling as to whether its use during a stipulated round would cause a player to be in breach of Rule 14–3. Such sample will become the property of the United States Golf Association for reference purposes. If a manufacturer fails to suit a sample before manufacturing and/or marketing the item, he assumes the risk of a ruling that use of the item would be contrary to the Rules of Golf.

Except as provided in the Rules, during a stipulated round the player shall not use any artificial device or unusual equipment:

a. Which might assist him in making a stroke or in his play; or

b. For the purpose of gauging or measuring distance or conditions which might affect his play; or

c. Which might assist him in gripping the club, except that:

(i) plain gloves may be worn;

(ii) resin, powder and drying or moisturizing agents may be used;

(iii) tape or gauze may be applied to the grip (provided such application does not render the grip non-conforming under Rule 4–1c); and

(iv) a towel or handkerchief may be wrapped around the grip.

Penalty for Breach of Rule 14–3: Disqualification.

14–4. Striking the Ball More than Once

If a player's club strikes the ball more than once in the course of a stroke, the player shall count the stroke and add a penalty stroke, making two strokes in all.

14–5. Playing Moving Ball

A player shall not play while his ball is moving.
Exceptions:
Ball falling off tee—Rule 11–3.
Striking the ball more than once—Rule 14–4.
Ball moving in water—Rule 14–6.
When the ball begins to move only after the player has begun the stroke or the backward movement of his club for the stroke, he shall incur no penalty under this Rule for playing a moving ball, but he is not exempt from any penalty incurred under the following Rules:
Ball at rest moved by player—Rule 18–2a.
Ball at rest moving after address—Rule 18–2b.
Ball at rest moving after loose impediment touched—Rule 18–2c.
(Ball purposely deflected or stopped by player, partner or caddie—see Rule 1–2.)

14–6. Ball Moving in Water

When a ball is moving in water in a water hazard, the player may, without penalty, make a stroke, but he must not delay making his stroke in order to allow the wind or current to improve the position of the ball. A ball moving in water in a water hazard may be lifted if the player elects to invoke Rule 26.

Penalty for Breach of Rule 14–5 or –6: Match play—
Loss of hole; Stroke play—Two strokes.

RULE 15. WRONG BALL;
SUBSTITUTED BALL

A "wrong ball" is any ball other than the player's:
a. Ball in play,
b. Provisional ball or
c. Second ball played under Rule 3–3 or Rule 20–7b in stroke play.

Note: Ball in play includes a ball substituted for the ball in play, whether or not such substitution is permitted.

15–1. General

A player must hole out with the ball played from the teeing ground unless a Rule permits him to substitute another ball. If a player substitutes another ball when not so permitted, that ball is not a wrong ball; it becomes the ball in play and, if the error is not corrected as provided in Rule 20–6, the player shall incur a penalty of loss of hole in match play or two strokes in stroke play.

(Playing from wrong place—see Rule 20–7.)

15–2. Match Play

If a player plays a stroke with a wrong ball except in a hazard, he shall lose the hole.

   If a player plays any strokes in a hazard with a wrong ball, there is no penalty. Strokes played in a hazard with a wrong ball do not count in the player's score. If the wrong ball belongs to another player, its owner shall place a ball on the spot from which the wrong ball was first played.

   If the player and opponent exchange balls during the play of a hole, the first to play the wrong ball other than from a hazard shall lose the hole; when this cannot be determined, the hole shall be played out with the balls exchanged.

15-3. Stroke Play

If a competitor plays a stroke or strokes with a wrong ball, he shall incur a penalty of two strokes, unless the only stroke or strokes played with such ball were played when it was in a hazard, in which case no penalty is incurred. The competitor must correct his mistake by playing the correct ball. If he fails to correct his mistake before he plays a stroke from the next teeing ground or, in the case of the last hole of the round, fails to declare his intention to correct his mistake before leaving the putting green, he shall be disqualified. Strokes played by a competitor with a wrong ball do not count in his score. If the wrong ball belongs to another competitor, its owner shall place a ball on the spot from which the wrong ball was first played.

RULE 16. PUTTING GREEN

The "putting green" is all ground of the hole being played which is specially prepared for putting or otherwise defined as such by the Committee. A ball is on the putting green when any part of it touches the putting green. The "line of putt" is the line which the player wishes his ball to take after a stroke on the putting green. Except with respect to Rule 16–1e, the line of putt includes a reasonable distance on either side of the intended line. The line of putt does not extend beyond the hole.

A ball is "holed" when it is at rest within the circumference of the hole and all of it is below the level of the lip of the hole.

16–1. General

a. Touching Line of Putt

The line of putt must not be touched except:

(i) the player may move sand and loose soil on the putting green and other loose impediments by picking them up or by brushing them aside with his hand or a club without pressing anything down;

(ii) in addressing the ball, the player may place the club in front of the ball without pressing anything down;

(iii) in measuring—Rule 10–4;

(iv) in lifting the ball—Rule 16–1b;

(v) in pressing down a ball-marker;

(vi) in repairing old hole plugs or ball marks on the putting green—Rule 16–1c; and

(vii) in removing movable obstructions—Rule 24–1.

(Indicating line for putting on putting green—see Rule 8–2b.)

b. Lifting Ball

A ball on the putting green may be lifted and, if desired, cleaned. A ball so lifted shall be replaced on the spot from which it was lifted.

c. Repair of Hole Plugs, Ball Marks and Other Damage

The player may repair an old hole plug or damage to the putting green caused by the impact of a ball, whether or not the player's ball lies on the putting green. If the ball is moved in the process of such repair, it shall be replaced, without penalty. Any other damage to the putting green shall not be repaired if it might assist the player in his subsequent play of the hole.

d. Testing Surface

During the play of a hole, a player shall not test the surface of the putting green by rolling a ball or roughening or scraping the surface.

e. Standing Astride or on Line of Putt

The player shall not make a stroke on the putting green from a stance astride, or with either foot touching, the line of putt or an extension of that line behind the ball.

f. Position of Caddie or Partner

While making a stroke on the putting green, the player shall not allow his caddie, his partner or his partner's caddie to position himself on or close to an extension of the line of putt behind the ball.

g. Playing Stroke While Another Ball in Motion

The player shall not play a stroke while another ball is in motion after a stroke from the putting green, except that, if a player does so, he incurs no penalty if it was his turn to play.

(Lifting ball interfering with or assisting play while another ball in motion—see Rule 22.)

Penalty for Breach of Rule 16–1: Match play—Loss of hole; Stroke play—Two strokes.

16–2. Ball Overhanging Hole

When any part of the ball overhangs the lip of the hole, the player is allowed enough time to reach the hole without unreasonable delay and an additional ten seconds to determine whether the ball is at rest.

If by then the ball has not fallen into the hole, it is deemed to be at rest. If the ball subsequently falls into the hole, the player is deemed to have holed out with his last stroke, and he shall add a penalty stroke to his score for the hole; otherwise there is no penalty under this Rule.

(Undue delay—see Rule 6–7.)

RULE 17. FLAGSTICK

17–1. Flagstick Attended, Removed or Held Up

Before and during the stroke, the player may have the flagstick attended, removed or held up to indicate the position of the hole. This may be done only on the authority of the player before he plays his stroke. If, prior to the stroke, the flagstick is attended, removed or held up by anyone with the player's knowledge and no objection is made, the player shall be deemed to have authorized it. If anyone attends or holds up the flagstick or stands near the hole while a stroke is being played, he shall be deemed to be attending the flagstick until the ball comes to rest.

17–2. Unauthorized Attendance

a. Match Play—In match play, an opponent or his caddie shall not, without the authority or prior knowledge of the player, attend, remove or hold up the flagstick while the player is making a stroke or his ball is in motion.

b. Stroke Play—In stroke play, if a fellow-competitor or his caddie attends, removes or holds up the flagstick without the competitor's authority or prior knowledge while the competitor is making a stroke or his ball is in motion, the fellow-competitor shall incur the penalty for breach of this Rule. In such circumstances, if the competitor's ball strikes the flagstick, the person attending it or anything carried by him, the competitor incurs no penalty and the ball shall be played as it lies, except that, if the stroke was played from the putting green, the stroke shall be cancelled, the ball replaced and the stroke replayed.

Penalty for Breach of Rule 17–1 or –2: Match play—Loss of hole;
Stroke play—Two strokes.

17–3. Ball Striking Flagstick or Attendant

The player's ball shall not strike:

a. The flagstick when attended, removed or held up by the player, his partner or either of their caddies, or by another person with the player's authority or prior knowledge; or

b. The player's caddie, his partner or his partner's caddie when attending the flagstick, or another person attending the flagstick with the player's authority or prior knowledge or anything carried by any such person; or

c. The flagstick in the hole, unattended, when the ball has been played from the putting green.

Penalty for Breach of Rule 17–3:

Match play—Loss of hole;

Stroke play— Two strokes and the ball shall be played as it lies.

17–4. Ball Resting Against Flagstick

If the ball rests against the flagstick when it is in the hole, the player or another person authorized by him may move or remove the flagstick and if the ball falls into the hole, the player shall be deemed to have holed out with his last stroke; otherwise, the ball, if moved, shall be placed on the lip of the hole, without penalty.

RULE 18. BALL AT REST

A ball is deemed to have "moved" if it leaves its position and comes to rest in any other place. An "outside agency" is any agency not part of the match or, in stroke play, not part of the competitor's side, and includes a referee, a marker, an observer and a forecaddie. Neither wind nor water is an outside agency. "Equipment" is anything used, worn or carried by or for the player except any ball he has played at the hole being played and any small object, such as a coin or a tee, when used to mark the position of a ball or the extent of an area in which a ball is to be dropped. Equipment includes a golf cart, whether or not motorized. If such a cart is shared by two or more players, the cart and everything in it are deemed to be the equipment of the player whose ball is involved except that, when the cart is being moved by one of the players sharing it, the cart and everything in it are deemed to be that player's equipment.

Note: A ball played at the hole being played is equipment when it has been lifted and not put back into play.

A player has "addressed the ball" when he has taken his stance and has also grounded his club, except that in a hazard a player has addressed the ball when he has taken his stance. Taking the "stance" consists in a player placing his feet in position for and preparatory to making a stroke.

18–1. By Outside Agency

If a ball at rest is moved by an outside agency, the player shall incur no penalty and the ball shall be replaced before the player plays another stroke.

(Player's ball at rest moved by another ball— see Rule 18–5.)

18-2. By Player, Partner, Caddie or Equipment

a. General

When a player's ball is in play, if:

(i) the player, his partner or either of their caddies lifts or moves it, touches it purposely (except with a club in the act of addressing it) or causes it to move except as permitted by a Rule, or

(ii) equipment of the player or his partner causes the ball to move, the player shall incur a penalty stroke. The ball shall be replaced unless the movement of the ball occurs after the player has begun his swing and he does not discontinue his swing. Under the Rules no penalty is incurred if a player accidentally causes his ball to move in the following circumstances:

in measuring to determine which ball farther from hole—Rule 10-4

In searching for covered ball in hazard or for ball in casual water, ground under repair, etc.—Rule 12-1

The process of repairing hole plug or ball mark—Rule 16-1c

In the process of removing loose impediment on putting green—Rule 18-2c

In the process of lifting ball under a Rule—Rule 20-1

In the process of placing or replacing ball under a Rule—Rule 20-3a

In removal of movable obstruction—Rule 24-1.

b. Ball Moving After Address

If a player's ball in play moves after he has addressed it (other than as a result of a stroke), the player shall be deemed to have moved the ball and shall incur a penalty stroke. The player shall replace the ball unless the movement of the ball occurs after he has begun his swing and he does not discontinue his swing.

c. Ball Moving After Loose Impediment Touched

Through the green, if the ball moves after any loose impediment lying within a club-length of it has been touched by the player, his partner or either of their caddies and before the player has addressed it, the player shall be deemed to have moved the ball and shall incur a penalty stroke. The player shall replace the ball unless the movement of the ball occurs after he has begun his swing and he does not discontinue his swing.

On the putting green, if the ball or the ball-marker moves in the process of removing any loose impediment, the ball or the ball-marker shall be replaced. There is no penalty provided the movement of the ball or the ball-marker is directly attributable to the removal of the loose impediment. Otherwise, the player shall incur a penalty stroke under Rule 18-2a or 20-1.

18–3. By Opponent, Caddie or Equipment in Match Play

a. During Search

If, during search for a player's ball, the ball is moved by an opponent, his caddie or his equipment, no penalty is incurred and the player shall replace the ball.

b. Other Than During Search

If, other than during search for a ball, the ball is touched or moved by an opponent, his caddie or his equipment, except as otherwise provided in the Rules, the opponent shall incur a penalty stroke. The player shall replace the ball.

(Ball moved in measuring to determine which ball farther from the hole —see Rule 10–4.)

(Playing a wrong ball—see Rule 15–2.)

18–4. By Fellow-Competitor, Caddie or Equipment in Stroke Play

If a competitor's ball is moved by a fellow-competitor, his caddie or his equipment, no penalty is incurred. The competitor shall replace his ball.

(Playing a wrong ball—see Rule 15–3.)

18–5. By Another Ball

If a ball in play and at rest is moved by another ball in motion after a stroke, the moved ball shall be replaced.

*Penalty for Breach of Rule: Match play—Loss of hole; Stroke play—Two strokes.

*If a player who is required to replace a ball fails to do so, he shall incur the general penalty for breach of Rule 18 but no additional penalty under Rule 18 shall be applied.

Note 1: If a ball to be replaced under this Rule is not immediately recoverable, another ball may be substituted.

Note 2: If it is impossible to determine the spot on which a ball is to be placed, see Rule 20–3c.

RULE 19. BALL IN
MOTION OR STOPPED

An "outside agency" is any agency not part of the match or, in stroke play, not part of the competitor's side, and includes a referee, a marker, an observer and a forecaddie. Neither wind nor water is an outside agency. "Equipment" is anything used, worn or carried by or for the player except any ball he has played at the hole being played and any small object, such as a coin or a tee, when used to mark the position of a ball or the extent of an area in which a ball is to be dropped. Equipment includes a golf cart, whether or not motorized. If such a cart is shared by two or more players, the cart and everything in it are deemed to be the equipment of the player whose ball is involved except that, when the cart is being moved by one of the players sharing it, the cart and everything in it are deemed to be that player's equipment.
Note: A ball played at the hole being played is equipment when it has been lifted and not put back into play.

19-1. By Outside Agency

If a ball in motion is accidentally deflected or stopped by any outside agency, it is a rub of the green, no penalty is incurred and the ball shall be played as it lies except:

a. If a ball in motion after a stroke other than on the putting green comes to rest in or on any moving or animate outside agency, the player shall, through the green or in a hazard, drop the ball, or on the putting green place the ball, as near as possible to the spot where the outside agency was when the ball came to rest in or on it, and

b. If a ball in motion after a stroke on the putting green is deflected or stopped by, or comes to rest in or on, any moving or animate outside agency except a worm or an insect, the stroke shall be cancelled, the ball replaced and the stroke replayed.

If the ball is not immediately recoverable, another ball may be substituted.

(Player's ball deflected or stopped by another ball - see Rule 19–5.)

Note: If the referee or the Committee determines that a player's ball has been purposely deflected or stopped by an outside agency, Rule 1–4 applies to the player. If the outside agency is a fellow-competitor or his caddie, Rule 1–2 applies to the fellow-competitor.

19–2. By Player, Partner, Caddie or Equipment

a. Match Play

If a player's ball is accidentally deflected or stopped by himself, his partner or either of their caddies or equipment, he shall lose the hole.

b. Stroke Play

If a competitor's ball is accidentally deflected or stopped by himself, his partner or either of their caddies or equipment, the competitor shall incur a penalty of two strokes. The ball shall be played as it lies, except when it comes to rest in or on the competitor's, his partner's or either of their caddies' clothes or equipment, in which case the competitor shall through the green or in a hazard drop the ball, or on the putting green place the ball, as near as possible to where the article was when the ball came to rest in or on it.

Exception: Dropped ball—see Rule 20–2a.

(Ball purposely deflected or stopped by player, partner or caddie—see Rule 1–2.)

19–4. By Fellow Competitor, Caddie or Equipment

Stroke Play See Rule 19–1 regarding ball deflected by outside agency.

19–5. By Another Ball

a. At Rest

If a player's ball in motion after a stroke is deflected or stopped by a ball in play and at rest, the player shall play his ball as it lies. In match play, no penalty is incurred. In stroke play, there is no penalty unless both balls lay on the putting green prior to the stroke, in which case the player incurs a penalty of two strokes.

b. In Motion

If a player's ball in motion after a stroke is deflected or stopped by another ball in motion after a stroke, the player shall play his ball as it lies. There is no penalty unless the player was in breach of Rule 16–1g, in which case he shall incur the penalty for breach of that Rule. Exception: If the player's ball is in motion after a stroke on the putting green and the other ball in motion is an outside agency—see Rule 19–1b.

Penalty for Breach of Rule:
Match play—Loss of hole;
Stroke play—Two strokes.

RULE 20. LIFTING, DROPPING & PLAYING FROM WRONG PLACE

20-1. Lifting

A ball to be lifted under the Rules may be lifted by the player, his partner or another person authorized by the player. In any such case, the player shall be responsible for any breach of the Rules. The position of the ball shall be marked before it is lifted under a Rule which requires it to be replaced. If it is not marked, the player shall incur a penalty of one stroke and the ball shall be replaced. If it is not replaced, the player shall incur the general penalty for breach of this Rule but no additional penalty under Rule 20–1 shall be applied.

If a ball or ball-marker is accidentally moved in the process of lifting the ball under a Rule or marking its position, the ball or the ball-marker shall be replaced. There is no penalty provided the movement of the ball or the ball-marker is directly attributable to the specific act of marking the position of or lifting the ball. Otherwise, the player shall incur a penalty stroke under this Rule or Rule 18–2a.

Exception: If a player incurs a penalty for failing to act in accordance with Rule 5–3 or 12–2, no additional penalty under Rule 20–1 shall be applied.

Note: The position of a ball to be lifted should be marked by placing a ball-marker, a small coin or other similar object immediately behind the ball. If the ball-marker interferes with the play, stance or stroke of another player, it should be placed one or more clubhead-lengths to one side.

20–2. Dropping and Re-dropping

a. By Whom and How

A ball to be dropped under the Rules shall be dropped by the player himself. He shall stand erect, hold the ball at shoulder height and arm's length and drop it. If a ball is dropped by any other person or in any other manner and the error is not corrected as provided in Rule 20–6, the player shall incur a penalty stroke.

If the ball touches the player, his partner, either of their caddies or their equipment before or after it strikes a part of the course, the ball shall be re-dropped, without penalty. There is no limit to the number of times a ball shall be re-dropped in such circumstances.

(Taking action to influence position or movement of ball—see Rule 1–2.)

b. Where to Drop

When a ball is to be dropped as near as possible to a specific spot, it shall be dropped not nearer the hole than the specific spot which, if it is not precisely known to the player, shall be estimated.

A ball when dropped must first strike a part of the course where the applicable Rule requires it to be dropped. If it is not so dropped, Rules 20–6 and –7 apply.

c. When to Re-Drop

A dropped ball shall be re-dropped without penalty if it:

(i) rolls into a hazard;

(ii) rolls out of a hazard;

(iii) rolls onto a putting green;

(iv) rolls out of bounds;

(v) rolls to a position where there is interference by the condition from which relief was taken under Rule 24–2 (immovable obstruction) or Rule 25–1 (abnormal ground conditions), or rolls back into the pitch-mark from which it was lifted under Rule 25–2 (embedded ball);

(vi) rolls and comes to rest more than two club-lengths from where it first struck a part of the course;

(vii) rolls and comes to rest nearer the hole than its original position or estimated position (see Rule 20–2b) unless otherwise permitted by the Rules; or

(viii) rolls and comes to rest nearer the hole than the point where the original ball last crossed the margin of the area or hazard, (Rule 25–1c(i) and (ii)) or the margin of the water hazard (Rule 26–1b) or lateral water hazard (Rule 26–1c).

If the ball when re-dropped rolls into any position listed above, it shall be placed as near as possible to the spot where it first struck a part of the course when re-dropped. If a ball to be re-dropped or placed under this Rule is not immediately recoverable, another ball may be substituted.

20–3. Placing and Replacing

a. By Whom and Where

A ball to be placed under the Rules shall be placed by the player or his partner. If a ball is to be replaced, the player, his partner or the person who lifted or moved it shall place it on the spot from which it was lifted or moved. In any such case, the player shall be responsible for any breach of the Rules.

If a ball or ball-marker is accidentally moved in the process of placing or replacing the ball, the ball or the ball-marker shall be replaced. There is no penalty provided the movement of the ball or the ball-marker is directly attributable to the specific act of placing or replacing the ball or removing the ball-marker. Otherwise, the player shall incur a penalty stroke under Rule 18–2a or 20–1.

b. Lie of Ball to Be Placed or Replaced Altered

If the original lie of a ball to be placed or replaced has been altered:

(i) except in a hazard, the ball shall be placed in the nearest lie most similar to the original lie which is not more than one club-length from the original lie not nearer the hole and not in a hazard;

(ii) in a water hazard, the ball shall be placed in accordance with Clause (i) above, except that the ball must be placed in the water hazard;

(iii) in a bunker, the original lie shall be recreated as nearly as possible and the ball shall be placed in that lie.

c. Spot Not Determinable

If it is impossible to determine the spot where the ball is to be placed or replaced:

(i) through the green, the ball shall be dropped as near as possible to the place where it lay but not in a hazard or on a putting green;

(ii) in a hazard, the ball shall be dropped in the hazard as near as possible to the place where it lay;

(iii) on the putting green, the ball shall be placed as near as possible to the place where it lay but not in a hazard.

d. Ball Fails To Come To Rest on Spot

If a ball when placed fails to come to rest on the spot on which it was placed, it shall be replaced without penalty.

If it still fails to come to rest on that spot:

(i) except in a hazard, it shall be placed at the nearest spot not nearer the hole or in a hazard where it can be placed at rest;

(ii) in a hazard, it shall be placed in the hazard at the nearest spot not nearer the hole where it can be placed at rest. If a ball when placed comes to rest on the spot on which it is placed, and it subsequently moves, there is no penalty and the ball shall be played as it lies, unless the provisions of any other Rule apply.

Penalty for Breach of Rule 20–1, –2 or –3:

Match play—Loss of hole; Stroke play—Two strokes.

20–4. When Ball Dropped or Placed Is in Play

If the player's ball in play has been lifted, it is again in play when dropped or placed.

A substituted ball becomes the ball in play when it has been dropped or placed. (Ball incorrectly substituted—see Rule 15–1.)

(Lifting ball incorrectly substituted, dropped or placed—see Rule 20–6.)

20–5. Playing Next Stroke from Where Previous Stroke Played

When, under the Rules, a player elects or is required to play his next stroke from where a previous stroke was played, he shall proceed as follows: if the stroke is to be played from the teeing ground, the ball to be played shall be played from anywhere within the teeing ground and may be teed;

if the stroke is to be played from through the green or a hazard, it shall be dropped;

if the stroke is to be played on the putting green, it shall be placed.

Penalty for Breach of Rule 20-5:
Match play—Loss of hole;
Stroke play—Two strokes.

20–6. Lifting Ball Incorrectly Substituted, Dropped or Placed

A ball incorrectly substituted, dropped or placed in a wrong place or otherwise not in accordance with the Rules but not played may be lifted, without penalty, and the player shall then proceed correctly.

20–7. Playing from Wrong Place
For a ball played from outside the teeing ground or from a wrong teeing ground—see Rule 11–4 and –5.

a. Match Play

If a player plays a stroke with a ball which has been dropped or placed in a wrong place, he shall lose the hole.

b. Stroke Play

If a competitor plays a stroke with his ball in play (i) which has been dropped or placed in a wrong place or (ii) which has been moved and not replaced in a case where the Rules require replacement, he shall, provided a serious breach has not occurred, incur the penalty prescribed by the applicable Rule and play out the hole with the ball.

If, after playing from a wrong place, a competitor becomes aware of that fact and believes that a serious breach may be involved, he may, provided he has not played a stroke from the next teeing ground or, in the case of the last hole of the round, left the putting green, declare that he will play out the hole with a second ball dropped or placed in accordance with the Rules. The competitor shall report the facts to the Committee before returning his score card; if he fails to do so, he shall be disqualified. The Committee shall determine whether a serious breach of the Rule occurred. If so, the score with the second ball shall count and the competitor shall add two penalty strokes to his score with that ball.

If a serious breach has occurred and the competitor has failed to correct it as prescribed above, he shall be disqualified.

Note: If a competitor plays a second ball, penalty strokes incurred by playing the ball ruled not to count and strokes subsequently taken with that ball shall be disregarded.

RULE 21. CLEANING

Rule 21. Cleaning Ball

A ball on the putting green may be cleaned when lifted under Rule 16–1b. Elsewhere, a ball may be cleaned when lifted except when it has been lifted:

a. To determine if it is unfit for play (Rule 5–3);

b. For identification (Rule 12-2), in which case it may be cleaned only to the extent necessary for identification; or

c. Because it is interfering with or assisting play (Rule 22).

If a player cleans his ball during play of a hole except as provided in this Rule, he shall incur a penalty of one stroke and the ball, if lifted, shall be replaced.

If a player who is required to replace a ball fails to do so, he shall incur the penalty for breach of Rule 20–3a, but no additional penalty under Rule 21 shall be applied.

Exception: If a player incurs a penalty for failing to act in accordance with Rule 5–3, 12–2 or 22, no additional penalty under Rule 21 shall be applied.

RULE 22. BALL
INTERFERING WITH OR ASSISTING PLAY

Rule 22. Ball Interfering with or Assisting Play

Any player may:

    a. Lift his ball if he considers that the ball might assist any other player or

    b. Have any other ball lifted if he considers that the ball might interfere with his play or assist the play of any other player, but this may not be done while another ball is in motion. In stroke play, a player required to lift his ball may play first rather than lift. A ball lifted under this Rule shall be replaced.

Penalty for Breach of Rule: Match play— Loss of hole; Stroke play —Two strokes.

Note: Except on the putting green, the ball may not be cleaned when lifted under this Rule—see Rule 21.

RULE 23. LOOSE
IMPEDIMENTS

"Loose impediments" are natural objects such as stones, leaves, twigs, branches and the like, dung, worms and insects and casts or heaps made by them, provided they are not fixed or growing, are not solidly embedded and do not adhere to the ball.
Sand and loose soil are loose impediments on the putting green but not elsewhere.

Snow and natural ice, other than frost, are either casual water or loose impediments, at the option of the player. Manufactured ice is an obstruction.

Dew and frost are not loose impediments.

23–1. Relief
Except when both the loose impediment and the ball lie in or touch the same hazard, any loose impediment may be removed without penalty. If the ball moves, see Rule 18–2c.

When a ball is in motion, a loose impediment which might influence the movement of the ball shall not be removed.
Penalty for Breach of Rule:
Match play—Loss of hole;
Stroke play—Two strokes.
(Searching for ball in hazard—
see Rule 12–1.)
(Touching line of putt—
see Rule 16–1a.)

RULE 24. OBSTRUCTIONS

An "obstruction" is anything artificial, including the artificial surfaces and sides of roads and paths and manufactured ice, except:

a. Objects defining out of bounds, such as walls, fences, stakes and railings;

b. Any part of an immovable artificial object which is out of bounds; and

c. Any construction declared by the Committee to be an integral part of the course.

24–1. Movable Obstruction

A player may obtain relief from a movable obstruction as follows:

a. If the ball does not lie in or on the obstruction, the obstruction may be removed. If the ball moves, it shall be replaced, and there is no penalty provided that the movement of the ball is directly attributable to the removal of the obstruction. Otherwise, Rule 18–2a applies.

b. If the ball lies in or on the obstruction, the ball may be lifted, without penalty, and the obstruction removed. The ball shall through the green or in a hazard be dropped, or on the putting green be placed, as near as possible to the spot directly under the place where the ball lay in or on the obstruction, but not nearer the hole. The ball may be cleaned when lifted under Rule 24–1.

When a ball is in motion, an obstruction which might influence the movement of the ball, other than an attended flagstick or equipment of the players, shall not be removed.

Note: If a ball to be dropped or placed under this Rule is not immediately recoverable, another ball may be substituted.

24–2. Immovable Obstruction

a. Interference

Interference by an immovable obstruction occurs when a ball lies in or on the obstruction, or so close to the obstruction that the obstruction interferes with the player's stance or the area of his intended swing. If the player's ball lies on the putting green, interference also occurs if an immovable obstruction on the putting green intervenes on his line of putt. Otherwise, intervention on the line of play is not, of itself, interference under this Rule.

b. Relief

Except when the ball is in a water hazard or a lateral water hazard, a player may obtain relief from interference by an immovable obstruction, without penalty, as follows:

(i) Through the Green: If the ball lies through the green, the point on the course nearest to where the ball lies shall be determined (without crossing over, through or under the obstruction) which (a) is not nearer the hole, (b) avoids interference (as defined) and (c) is not in a hazard or on a putting green. The player shall lift the ball and drop it within one club-length of the point thus determined on a part of the course which fulfils (a), (b) and (c) above. Note: The prohibition against crossing over, through or under the obstruction does not apply to the artificial surfaces and sides of roads and paths or when the ball lies in or on the obstruction.

(ii) In a Bunker: If the ball is in a bunker, the player shall lift and drop the ball in accordance with Clause (i) above, except that the ball must be dropped in the bunker.

(iii) On the Putting Green: If the ball lies on the putting green, the player shall lift the ball and place it in the nearest position to where it lay which affords relief from interference, but not nearer the hole nor in a hazard. The ball may be cleaned when lifted under Rule 24–2b.

(Ball rolling to a position where there is interference by the condition from which relief was taken—see Rule 20–2c(v).)

Exception: A player may not obtain relief under Rule 24–2b if (a) it is clearly unreasonable for him to play a stroke because of interference by anything other than an immovable obstruction or (b) interference by an immovable obstruction would occur only through use of an unnecessarily abnormal stance, swing or direction of play.

Note 1: If a ball is in a water hazard (including a lateral water hazard), the player is not entitled to relief without penalty from interference by an immovable obstruction. The player shall play the ball as it lies or proceed under Rule 26–1.

Note 2: If a ball to be dropped or placed under this Rule is not immediately recoverable, another ball may be substituted.

c. Ball Lost

Except in a water hazard or a lateral water hazard, if there is reasonable evidence that a ball is lost in an immovable obstruction, the player may, without penalty, substitute another ball and follow the procedure prescribed in Rule 24–2b.

For the purpose of applying this Rule, the ball shall be deemed to lie at the spot where it entered the obstruction. If the ball is lost in an underground drain pipe or culvert the entrance to which is in a hazard, a ball must be dropped in that hazard or the player may proceed under Rule 26–1, if applicable.

Penalty for Breach of Rule: Match play—Loss of hole; Stroke play—Two strokes.

RULE 25. ABNORMAL
GROUND CONDITIONS & WRONG PUTTING GREEN

DEFINITION

"Casual water" is any temporary accumulation of water on the course which is visible before or after the player takes his stance and is not in a water hazard. Snow and natural ice, other than frost, are casual water or loose impediments, at the option of the player. Manufactured ice is an obstruction. Dew and frost are not casual water. A ball is in casual water when it lies in or any part of it touches the casual water.

"Ground under repair" is any portion of the course so marked by order of the Committee or so declared by its authorized representative. It includes material piled for removal and a hole made by a greenkeeper, even if not so marked. Stakes and lines defining ground under repair are in such ground. Stakes defining ground under repair are obstructions. The margin of ground under repair extends vertically downwards, but not upwards. A ball is in ground under repair when it lies in or any part of it touches the ground under repair.

Note 1: Grass cuttings and other material left on the course which have been abandoned and are not intended to be removed are not ground under repair unless so marked.

Note 2: The Committee may make a Local Rule prohibiting play from ground under repair or an environmentally-sensitive area which has been defined as ground under repair.

25–1. Casual Water, Ground Under Repair and Certain Damage to Course

a. Interference

Interference by casual water, ground under repair or a hole, cast or runway made by a burrowing animal, a reptile or a bird occurs when a ball lies in or touches any of these conditions or when such a condition on the course interferes with the player's stance or the area of his intended swing.

If the player's ball lies on the putting green, interference also occurs if such condition on the putting green intervenes on his line of putt.

If interference exists, the player may either play the ball as it lies (unless prohibited by Local Rule) or take relief as provided in Clause b.

Note: The Committee may make a Local Rule denying the player relief from interference with his stance by all or any of the conditions covered by this Rule.

b. Relief

If the player elects to take relief, he shall proceed as follows:

(i) Through the Green: If the ball lies through the green, the point on the course nearest to where the ball lies shall be determined which (a) is not nearer the hole, (b) avoids interference by the condition, and (c) is not in a hazard or on a putting green. The player shall lift the ball and drop it without penalty within one club-length of the point thus determined on a part of the course which fulfils (a), (b) and (c) above.

(ii) In a Hazard: If the ball is in a hazard, the player shall lift and drop the ball either:

(a) Without penalty, in the hazard, as near as possible to the spot where the ball lay, but not nearer the hole, on a part of the course which affords maximum available relief from the condition; or

(b) Under penalty of one stroke, outside the hazard, keeping the point where the ball lay directly between the hole and the spot on which the ball is dropped, with no limit to how far behind the hazard the ball may be dropped.

Exception: If a ball is in a water hazard (including a lateral water hazard), the player is not entitled to relief without penalty from a hole, cast or runway made by a burrowing animal, a reptile or a bird. The player shall play the ball as it lies or proceed under Rule 26–1

(iii) On the Putting Green: If the ball lies on the putting green, the player shall lift the ball and place it without penalty in the nearest position to where it lay which affords maximum available relief from the condition, but not nearer the hole nor in a hazard. The ball may be cleaned when lifted under Rule 25–1b. (Ball rolling to a position where there is interference by the condition from which relief was taken—see Rule 20–2c(v).)

cont . . .

cont . . . Exception: A player may not obtain relief under Rule 25–1b if (a) it is clearly unreasonable for him to play a stroke because of interference by anything other than a condition covered by Rule 25–1a or (b) interference by such a condition would occur only through use of an unnecessarily abnormal stance, swing or direction of play.

Note: If a ball to be dropped or placed under this Rule is not immediately recoverable, another ball may be substituted.

c. Ball Lost Under Condition Covered by Rule 25–1

It is a question of fact whether a ball lost after having been struck toward a condition covered by Rule 25–1 is lost under such condition. In order to treat the ball as lost under such condition, there must be reasonable evidence to that effect. In the absence of such evidence, the ball must be treated as a lost ball and Rule 27 applies.

(i) Outside a Hazard—If a ball is lost outside a hazard under a condition covered by Rule 25–1, the player may take relief as follows: the point on the course nearest to where the ball last crossed the margin of the area shall be determined which (a) is not nearer the hole than where the ball last crossed the margin, (b) avoids interference by the condition and (c) is not in a hazard or on a putting green. He shall drop a ball without penalty within one club-length of the point thus determined on a part of the course which fulfils (a), (b) and (c) above.

(ii) In a Hazard—If a ball is lost in a hazard under a condition covered by Rule 25–1, the player may drop a ball either:

(a) Without penalty, in the hazard, as near as possible to the point at which the original ball last crossed the margin of the area, but not nearer the hole, on a part of the course which affords maximum available relief from the condition or

(b) Under penalty of one stroke, outside the hazard, keeping the point at which the original ball last crossed the margin of the hazard directly between the hole and the spot on which the ball is dropped, with no limit to how far behind the hazard the ball may be dropped.

Exception: If a ball is in a water hazard (including a lateral water hazard), the player is not entitled to relief without penalty for a ball lost in a hole, cast or runway made by a burrowing animal, a reptile or a bird. The player shall proceed under Rule 26–1.

25–2. Embedded Ball

A ball embedded in its own pitch-mark in the ground in any closely mown area through the green may be lifted, cleaned and dropped, without penalty, as near as possible to the spot where it lay but not nearer the hole. The ball when dropped must first strike a part of the course through the green. "Closely mown area" means any area of the course, including paths through the rough, cut to fairway height or less.

25–3. Wrong Putting Green

A player must not play a ball which lies on a putting green other than that of the hole being played. The ball must be lifted and the player must proceed as follows: The point on the course nearest to where the ball lies shall be determined which (a) is not nearer the hole and (b) is not in a hazard or on a putting green. The player shall lift the ball and drop it without penalty within one club-length of the point thus determined on a part of the course which fulfils (a) and (b) above. The ball may be cleaned when so lifted.

Note: Unless otherwise prescribed by the Committee, the term "a putting green other than that of the hole being played"' includes a practice putting green or pitching green on the course.

Penalty for Breach of Rule: Match play—Loss of hole; Stroke play—Two strokes.

RULE 26. WATER HAZARDS (INCLUDING LATERAL WATER HAZARDS

DEFINITION

A "water hazard" is any sea, lake, pond, river, ditch, surface drainage ditch or other open water course (whether or not containing water) and anything of a similar nature. All ground or water within the margin of a water hazard is part of the water hazard. The margin of a water hazard extends vertically upwards and downwards. Stakes and lines defining the margins of water hazards are in the hazards. Such stakes are obstructions. A ball is in a water hazard when it lies in or any part of it touches the water hazard.

Note 1: Water hazards (other than lateral water hazards) should be defined by yellow stakes or lines.

Note 2: The Committee may make a Local Rule prohibiting play from an environmentally-sensitive area which has been defined as a water hazard.

A "lateral water hazard" is a water hazard or that part of a water hazard so situated that it is not possible or is deemed by the Committee to be impracticable to drop a ball behind the water hazard in accordance with Rule 26–1b.

That part of a water hazard to be played as a lateral water hazard should be distinctively marked. A ball is in a lateral water hazard when it lies in or any part of it touches the lateral water hazard.

Note 1: Lateral water hazards should be defined by red stakes or lines.

Note 2: The Committee may make a Local Rule prohibiting play from an environmentally-sensitive area which has been defined as a lateral water hazard.

26–1. Ball in Water Hazard

It is a question of fact whether a ball lost after having been struck toward a water hazard is lost inside or outside the hazard. In order to treat the ball as lost in the hazard, there must be reasonable evidence that the ball lodged in it. In the absence of such evidence, the ball must be treated as a lost ball and Rule 27 applies.

If a ball is in or is lost in a water hazard (whether the ball lies in water or not), the player may under penalty of one stroke:

a. Play a ball as nearly as possible at the spot from which the original ball was last played (see Rule 20–5); or

b. Drop a ball behind the water hazard, keeping the point at which the original ball last crossed the margin of the water hazard directly between the hole and the spot on which the ball is dropped, with no limit to how far behind the water hazard the ball may be dropped. or

c. As additional options available only if the ball last crossed the margin of a lateral water hazard, drop a ball outside the water hazard within two club-lengths of and not nearer the hole than (i) the point where the original ball last crossed the margin of the water hazard or (ii) a point on the opposite margin of the water hazard equidistant from the hole.

The ball may be cleaned when lifted under this Rule.

(Ball moving in water in a water hazard—see Rule 14–6.)

26–2. Ball Played Within Water Hazard

a. Ball Comes To Rest in The Hazard

If a ball played from within a water hazard comes to rest in the same hazard after the stroke, the player may:

(i) proceed under Rule 26–1; or

(ii) under penalty of one stroke, play a ball as nearly as possible at the spot from which the last stroke from outside the hazard was played (see Rule 20–5).

If the player proceeds under Rule 26–1a, he may elect not to play the dropped ball. If he so elects, he may:

a. Proceed under Rule 26–1b, adding the additional penalty of one stroke prescribed by that Rule; or

b. Proceed under Rule 26–1c, if applicable, adding the additional penalty of one stroke prescribed by that Rule; or

c. Add an additional penalty of one stroke and play a ball as nearly as possible at the spot from which the last stroke from outside the hazard was played (see Rule 20–5).

b. Ball Lost or Unplayable Outside Hazard or Out of Bounds

If a ball played from within a water hazard is lost or declared unplayable outside the hazard or is out of bounds, the player, after taking a penalty of one stroke under Rule 27–1 or 28a, may:

play a ball as nearly as possible at the spot in the hazard from which the original ball was last played (see Rule 20–5);or

(ii) proceed under Rule 26–1b, or if applicable Rule 26–1c, adding the additional penalty of one stroke prescribed by the Rule and using as the reference point the point where the original ball last crossed the margin of the hazard before it came to rest in the hazard; or

(iii) add an additional penalty of one stroke and play a ball as nearly as possible at the spot from which the last stroke from outside the hazard was played (see Rule 20–5).

Note 1: When proceeding under Rule 26–2b, the player is not required to drop a ball under Rule 27–1 or 28a. If he does drop a ball, he is not required to play it. He may alternatively proceed under Clause (ii) or (iii).

Note 2: If a ball played from within a water hazard is declared unplayable outside the hazard, nothing in Rule 26–2b precludes the player from proceeding under Rule 28b or c.

Penalty for Breach of Rule: Match play—Loss of hole; Stroke play—Two strokes.

RULE 27. BALL LOST
OR OUT OF BOUNDS; PROVISIONAL BALL

A ball is "lost" if:

a. It is not found or identi-fied as his by the player within five minutes after the player's side or his or their caddies have begun to search for it; or

b. The player has put another ball into play under the Rules, even though he may not have searched for the original ball; or

c. The player has played any stroke with a provisional ball from the place where the original ball is likely to be or from a point nearer the hole than that place, where-upon the provisional ball becomes the ball in play.

Time spent in playing a wrong ball is not counted in the five-minute period allowed for search.

"Out of bounds" is ground on which play is prohibited.

When out of bounds is defined by reference to stakes or a fence, or as being beyond stakes or a fence, the out of bounds line is determined by the nearest inside points of the stakes or fence posts at ground level excluding angled supports.

When out of bounds is defined by a line on the ground, the line itself is out of bounds.

The out of bounds line extends vertically upwards and downwards. A ball is out of bounds when all of it lies out of bounds.

A player may stand out of bounds to play a ball lying within bounds.

A "provisional ball" is a ball played under Rule 27–2 for a ball which may be lost outside a water hazard or may be out of bounds.

DEFINITION

If the original ball is lost in an immovable obstruction (Rule 24–2) or under a condition covered by Rule 25–1 (casual water, ground under repair and certain damage to the course), the player may proceed under the applicable Rule. If the original ball is lost in a water hazard, the player shall proceed under Rule 26. Such Rules may not be used unless there is reasonable evidence that the ball is lost in an immovable obstruction, under a condition covered by Rule 25–1 or in a water hazard.

27–1. Ball Lost or Out of Bounds

If a ball is lost outside a water hazard or is out of bounds, the player shall play a ball, under penalty of one stroke, as nearly as possible at the spot from which the original ball was last played (see Rule 20–5). Penalty for Breach of Rule 27–1 Match play—Loss of hole; Stroke play—Two strokes.

27-2. Provisional Ball

a. Procedure

If a ball may be lost outside a water hazard or may be out of bounds, to save time the player may play another ball provisionally as nearly as possible at the spot from which the original ball was played (see Rule 20–5). The player shall inform his opponent in match play or his marker or a fellow-competitor in stroke play that he intends to play a provisional ball, and he shall play it before he or his partner goes forward to search for the original ball. If he fails to do so and plays another ball, such ball is not a provisional ball and becomes the ball in play under penalty of stroke and distance (Rule 27–1); the original ball is deemed to be lost.

b. When Provisional Ball Becomes Ball in Play

The player may play a provisional ball until he reaches the place where the original ball is likely to be. If he plays a stroke with the provisional ball from the place where the original ball is likely to be or from a point nearer the hole than that place, the original ball is deemed to be lost and the provisional ball becomes the ball in play under penalty of stroke and distance (Rule 27–1).

If the original ball is lost outside a water hazard or is out of bounds, the provisional ball becomes the ball in play, under penalty of stroke and distance (Rule 27–1).

c. When Provisional Ball to Be Abandoned

If the original ball is neither lost outside a water hazard nor out of bounds, the player shall abandon the provisional ball and continue play with the original ball. If he fails to do so, any further strokes played with the provisional ball shall constitute playing a wrong ball and the provisions of Rule 15 shall apply.

Note: If the original ball is in a water hazard, the player shall play the ball as it lies or proceed under Rule 26. If it is lost in a water hazard or unplayable the player shall proceed under Rule 26 or 28, whichever is applicable.

RULE 28. LOOSE
IMPEDIMENTS

Rule 28. Ball Unplayable

The player may declare his ball unplayable at any place on the course except when the ball is in a water hazard. The player is the sole judge as to whether his ball is unplayable.

If the player deems his ball to be unplayable, he shall, under penalty of one stroke:

a. Play a ball as nearly as possible at the spot from which the original ball was last played (see Rule 20–5); or

b. Drop a ball within two club-lengths of the spot where the ball lay, but not nearer the hole; or

c. Drop a ball behind the point where the ball lay, keeping that point directly between the hole and the spot on which the ball is dropped, with no limit to how far behind that point the ball may be dropped.

If the unplayable ball is in a bunker, the player may proceed under Clause a, b or c. If he elects to proceed under Clause b or c, a ball must be dropped in the bunker.

The ball may be cleaned when lifted under this Rule.

Penalty for Breach of Rule:
Match play—Loss of hole;
Stroke play—Two strokes.

RULE 29. THREESOMES
& FOURSOMES

Threesome: A match in which one plays against two, and each side plays one ball. Foursome: A match in which two play against two, and each side plays one ball.

29–1. General

In a threesome or a foursome, during any stipulated round the partners shall play alternately from the teeing grounds and alternately during the play of each hole. Penalty strokes do not affect the order of play.

29–2. Match Play

If a player plays when his partner should have played, his side shall lose the hole.

29–3. Stroke Play

If the partners play a stroke or strokes in incorrect order, such stroke or strokes shall be cancelled and the side shall incur a penalty of two strokes. The side shall correct the error by playing a ball in correct order as nearly as possible at the spot from which it first played in incorrect order (see Rule 20–5). If the side plays a stroke from the next teeing ground without first correcting the error or, in the case of the last hole of the round, leaves the putting green without declaring its intention to correct the error, the side shall be disqualified.

RULE 30. THREE-BALL,
BEST-BALL & FOUR-BALL MATCH PLAY

Three-Ball: A match play competition in which three play against one another, each playing his own ball. Each player is playing two distinct matches.
Best-Ball: A match in which one plays against the better ball of two or the best ball of three players.
Four-Ball: A match in which two play their better ball against the better ball of two other players.

30–1. Rules of Golf Apply

The Rules of Golf, so far as they are not at variance with the following special Rules, shall apply to three-ball, best-ball and four-ball matches.

30–2. Three-Ball Match Play

a. Ball at Rest Moved by an Opponent

Except as otherwise provided in the Rules, if the player's ball is touched or moved by an opponent, his caddie or equipment other than during search, Rule 18–3b applies. That opponent shall incur a penalty stroke in his match with the player, but not in his match with the other opponent.

b. Ball Deflected or Stopped by an Opponent Accidentally

If a player's ball is accidentally deflected or stopped by an opponent, his caddie or equipment, no penalty shall be incurred. In his match with that opponent the player may play the ball as it lies or, before another stroke is played by either side, he may cancel the stroke and play a ball without penalty as nearly as possible at the spot from which the original ball was last played (see Rule 20–5). In his match with the other opponent, the ball shall be played as it lies.

Exception: Ball striking person attending flagstick—see Rule 17–3b.
(Ball purposely deflected or stopped by opponent—see Rule 1–2.)

30-3. Best-Ball and Four-Ball Match Play

a. Representation of Side

A side may be represented by one partner for all or any part of a match; all partners need not be present. An absent partner may join a match between holes, but not during play of a hole.

b. Maximum of Fourteen Clubs

The side shall be penalized for a breach of Rule 4-4 by any partner.

c. Order of Play

Balls belonging to the same side may be played in the order the side considers best.

d. Wrong Ball

If a player plays a stroke with a wrong ball except in a hazard, he shall be disqualified for that hole, but his partner incurs no penalty even if the wrong ball belongs to him. If the wrong ball belongs to another player, its owner shall place a ball on the spot from which the wrong ball was first played.

e. Disqualification of Side

(i) A side shall be disqualified for a breach of any of the following by any partner:

Rule 1–3—Agreement to Waive Rules.
Rule 4–1, –2 or –3—Clubs.
Rule 5–1 or –2—The Ball.
Rule 6–2a—Handicap (playing off higher handicap).
Rule 6–4—Caddie.
Rule 6–7—Undue Delay; Slow Play (repeated offense).
Rule 14–3—Artificial Devices and Unusual Equipment.

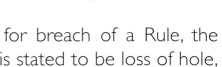

(ii) A side shall be disqualified for a breach of any of the following by all partners:

Rule 6–3—Time of Starting and Groups.
Rule 6–8—Discontinuance of Play.

f. Effect of Other Penalties

If a player's breach of a Rule assists his partner's play or adversely affects an opponent's play, the partner incurs the applicable penalty in addition to any penalty incurred by the player.

In all other cases where a player incurs a penalty for breach of a Rule, the penalty shall not apply to his partner. Where the penalty is stated to be loss of hole, the effect shall be to disqualify the player for that hole.

g. Another Form of Match Played Concurrently

In a best-ball or four-ball match when another form of match is played concurrently, the above special Rules shall apply.

RULE 31. FOUR-BALL
STROKE PLA

In four-ball stroke play two competitors play as partners, each playing his own ball. The lower score of the partners is the score for the hole. If one partner fails to complete the play of a hole, there is no penalty.

31–1. Rules of Golf Apply

The Rules of Golf, so far as they are not at variance with the following special Rules, shall apply to four-ball stroke play.

31–2. Representation of Side

A side may be represented by either partner for all or any part of a stipulated round; both partners need not be present. An absent competitor may join his partner between holes, but not during play of a hole.

31–3. Maximum of Fourteen Clubs

The side shall be penalized for a breach of Rule 4–4 by either partner.

31–4. Scoring

The marker is required to record for each hole only the gross score of whichever partner's score is to count. The gross scores to count must be individually identifiable; otherwise the side shall be disqualified. Only one of the partners need be responsible for complying with Rule 6–6b. (Wrong score—see Rule 31–7a.)

31–5. Order of Play

Balls belonging to the same side may be played in the order the side considers best.

31–6. Wrong Ball

If a competitor plays a stroke or strokes with a wrong ball except in a hazard, he shall add two penalty strokes to his score for the hole and shall then play the correct ball. His partner incurs no penalty even if the wrong ball belongs to him.

   If the wrong ball belongs to another competitor, its owner shall place a ball on the spot from which the wrong ball was first played.

31–7. Disqualification Penalties
a. Breach by One Partner

A side shall be disqualified from the competition for a breach of any of the following by either partner:
Rule 1–3—Agreement to Waive Rules. Rule 3–4—Refusal to Comply with Rule.
Rule 4–1, –2 or –3—Clubs. Rule 5–1 or –2—The Ball.
Rule 6–2b—Handicap (playing off higher handicap; failure to record handicap).
Rule 6–4—Caddie. Rule 6–6b—Signing and Returning Card.
Rule 6–6d—Wrong Score for Hole, i.e., when the recorded score of the partner whose score is to count is lower than actually taken. If the recorded score of the partner whose score is to count is higher than actually taken, it must stand as returned.
Rule 6–7—Undue Delay; Slow Play (repeated offense). Rule 7–1—Practice Before or Between Rounds.
Rule 14–3—Artificial Devices and Unusual Equipment. Rule 31–4—
Gross Scores to Count Not Individually Identifiable.

b. Breach by Both Partners
A side shall be disqualified:
(i) for a breach by both partners of Rule 6–3 (Time of Starting and Groups)
or Rule 6–8 (Discontinuance of Play), or
(ii) if, at the same hole, each partner is in breach of a Rule the penalty
for which is disqualification from the competition or for a hole.

c. For the Hole Only
In all other cases where a breach of a Rule would entail disqualification,
the competitor shall be disqualified only for the hole at which the breach occurred.

31–8. Effect of Other Penalties

If a competitor's breach of a Rule assists his partner's play, the partner incurs the applicable penalty in addition to any penalty incurred by the competitor.
In all other cases where a competitor incurs a penalty for breach of a Rule, the penalty shall not apply to his partner.

RULE 32. BOGEY, PAR
& STABLEFORD COMPETITIONS

32–1. Conditions

Bogey, par and Stableford competitions are forms of stroke competition in which play is against a fixed score at each hole. The Rules for stroke play, so far as they are not at variance with the following special Rules, apply.

a. Bogey and Par Competitions

The reckoning for bogey and par competitions is made as in match play. Any hole for which a competitor makes no return shall be regarded as a loss. The winner is the competitor who is most successful in the aggregate of holes. The marker is responsible for marking only the gross number of strokes for each hole where the competitor makes a net score equal to or less than the fixed score.
Note: Maximum of 14 clubs. Penalties as in match play—see Rule 4–4.

b. Stableford Competitions

The reckoning in Stableford competitions is made by points awarded in relation to a fixed score at each hole as follows:
Hole Played In Points
More than one over fixed score or no score returned—0
One over fixed score—1
Fixed score—2
One under fixed score—3
Two under fixed score—4
Three under fixed score—5
Four under fixed score— 6

The winner is the competitor who scores the highest number of points.

The marker shall be responsible for marking only the gross number of strokes at each hole where the competitor's net score earns one or more points.

 Note: Maximum of 14 clubs (Rule 4–4)—Penalties applied as follows:
From total points scored for the round, deduction of two points for each hole at which any breach occurred; maximum deduction per round: four points.

32–2. Disqualification Penalties

a. From the Competition
A competitor shall be disqualified from the competition for a breach of any of the following:
Rule 1–3—Agreement to Waive Rules.
Rule 3–4—Refusal to Comply with Rule.
Rule 4–1, –2 or –3—Clubs.
Rule 5–1 or –2—The Ball.
Rule 6–2b—Handicap (playing off higher handicap; failure to record handicap).
Rule 6–3—Time of Starting and Groups.
Rule 6–4—Caddie.
Rule 6–6b—Signing and Returning Card.
Rule 6–6d—Wrong Score for Hole, except that no penalty shall be incurred when a breach of this Rule does not affect the result of the hole.
Rule 6–7—Undue Delay; Slow Play (repeated offense).
Rule 6–8—Discontinuance of Play.
Rule 7–1—Practice Before or Between Rounds.
Rule 14–3—Artificial Devices and Unusual Equipment.
b. For a Hole
In all other cases where a breach of a Rule would entail disqualification, the competitor shall be disqualified only for the hole at which the breach occurred.

RULE 33. COMMITTEE

33–1. Conditions; Waiving Rule

The Committee shall lay down the conditions under which a competition is to be played.
The Committee has no power to waive a Rule of Golf.
Certain special rules governing stroke play are so substantially different from those governing match play that combining the two forms of play is not practicable and is not permitted. The results of matches played and the scores returned in these circumstances shall not be accepted
In stroke play the Committee may limit a referee's duties.

33–2. The Course

a. Defining Bounds and Margins

The Committee shall define accurately:

(i) the course and out of bounds,

(ii) the margins of water hazards and lateral water hazards,

(iii) ground under repair, and

(iv) obstructions and integral parts of the course.

b. New Holes

New holes should be made on the day on which a stroke competition begins and at such other times as the Committee considers necessary, provided all competitors in a single round play with each hole cut in the same position
Exception: When it is impossible for a damaged hole to be repaired so that it conforms with the Definition, the Committee may make a new hole in a nearby similar position.
Note: Where a single round is to be played on more than one day, the Committee may provide in the conditions of a competition that the holes and teeing grounds may be differently situated on each day of the competition, provided that, on any one day, all competitors play with each hole and each teeing ground in the same position.

c. Practice Ground

Where there is no practice ground available outside the area of a competition course, the Committee should lay down the area on which players may practice on any day of a competition, if it is practicable to do so. On any day of a stroke competition, the Committee should not normally permit practice on or to a putting green or from a hazard of the competition course.

d. Course Unplayable

If the Committee or its authorized representative considers that for any reason the course is not in a playable condition or that there are circumstances which render the proper playing of the game impossible, it may, in match play or stroke play, order a temporary suspension of play or, in stroke play, declare play null and void and cancel all scores for the round in question. When play has been temporarily suspended, it shall be resumed from where it was discontinued, even though resumption occurs on a subsequent day. When a round is cancelled, all penalties incurred in that round are cancelled. Procedure in discontinuing play—see Rule 6–8.)

33–3. Times of Starting and Groups

The Committee shall lay down the times of starting and, in stroke play, arrange the groups in which competitors shall play. When a match play competition is played over an extended period, the Committee shall lay down the limit of time within which each round shall be completed. When players are allowed to arrange the date of their match within these limits, the Committee should announce that the match must be played at a stated time on the last day of the period unless the players agree to a prior date.

33–4. Handicap Stroke Table

The Committee shall publish a table indicating the order of holes at which handicap strokes are to be given or received.

33-5. Score Card

In stroke play, the Committee shall issue for each competitor a score card containing the date and the competitor's name or, in foursome or four-ball stroke play, the competitors' names. In stroke play, the Committee is responsible for the addition of scores and application of the handicap recorded on the card.

In four-ball stroke play, the Committee is responsible for recording the better-ball score for each hole and in the process applying the handicaps recorded on the card, and adding the better-ball scores.

In bogey, par and Stableford competitions, the Committee is responsible for applying the handicap recorded on the card and determining the result of each hole and the overall result or points total.

33–6. Decision of Ties

The Committee shall announce the manner, day and time for the decision of a halved match or of a tie, whether played on level terms or under handicap. A halved match shall not be decided by stroke play. A tie in stroke play shall not be decided by a match.

33–7. Disqualification Penalty; Committee Discretion

A penalty of disqualification may in exceptional individual cases be waived, modified or imposed if the Committee considers such action warranted.

Any penalty less than disqualification shall not be waived or modified.

33–8. Local Rules

a. Policy

The Committee may make and publish Local Rules for abnormal conditions if they are consistent with the policy of the Governing Authority for the country concerned as set forth in Appendix I to these Rules.

b. Waiving Penalty

A penalty imposed by a Rule of Golf shall not be waived by a Local Rule.

RULE 34. DISPUTES &

34–1. Claims and Penalties

a. Match Play

In match play if a claim is lodged with the Committee under Rule 2–5, a decision should be given as soon as possible so that the state of the match may, if necessary, be adjusted.

If a claim is not made within the time limit provided by Rule 2-5, it shall not be considered unless it is based on facts previously unknown to the player making the claim and the player making the claim had been given wrong information (Rules 6–2a and 9) by an opponent. In any case, no later claim shall be considered after the result of the match has been officially announced, unless the Committee is satisfied that the opponent knew he was giving wrong information.

There is no time limit on applying the disqualification penalty for a breach of Rule 1–3.

b. Stroke Play

Except as provided below, in stroke play, no penalty shall be rescinded, modified or imposed after the competition has closed. A competition is deemed to have closed when the result has been officially announced or, in stroke play qualifying followed by match play, when the player has teed off in his first match.

Exceptions: A penalty of disqualification shall be imposed after the competition has closed if a competitor:

(i) was in breach of Rule 1–3 (Agreement to Waive Rules); or

(ii) returned a score card on which he had recorded a handicap which, before the competition closed, he knew was higher than that to which he was entitled, and this affected the number of strokes received (Rule 6–2b); or

(iii) returned a score for any hole lower than actually taken (Rule 6–6d) for any reason other than failure to include a penalty which, before the competition closed, he did not know he had incurred; or

(iv) knew, before the competition closed, that he had been in breach of any other Rule for which he prescribed penalty is disqualification.

138
GOLF SCHOOL

If a referee has been appointed by the Committee, his decision shall be final.

34–3. Committee's Decision

In the absence of a referee, any dispute or doubtful point on the Rules shall be referred to the Committee, whose decision shall be final.

If the Committee cannot come to a decision, it shall refer the dispute or doubtful point to the Rules of Golf Committee of the United States Golf Association, whose decision shall be final.
If the dispute or doubtful point has not been referred to the Rules of Golf Committee, the player or players have the right to refer an agreed statement through the Secretary of the Club to the Rules of Golf Committee for an opinion as to the correctness of the decision given.
The reply will be sent to the Secretary of the Club or Clubs concerned.

If play is conducted other than in accordance with the Rules of Golf, the Rules of Golf Committee will not give a decision on any question.

The EQUIPMENT

INTRODUCTION

Modern golf club designs would certainly baffle the long-ago swingers of whittled tree branches and the like. Imagine the incredulous gaze of the early golf ball maker, toting his top hat full of feathers and little leather pouch, upon the isododecahedron dimple pattern wrought upon some of today's four-piece spheres. As all things in the game, advances in equipment design have improved vastly the novice's ability to propel his or her projectile further and on a steadier path. The progress has been so rapid and awe-inspiring, the United States Golf Association and the Royal & Ancient devote a good deal of their combined efforts to qualifying new designs as legal or not for tournament play.

The choices presented today are so completely wide ranging that the modern golfer must devote nearly as much effort into selecting the proper equipment for his or her game as honing the swing itself. A brief review of golf's tools is helpful in this endeavor.

Of Bows and Horseshoes

Not surprisingly, the first record of a golf transaction comes from Scotland. It is the 15th century order of James IV requisitioning a set of clubs and balls from a wood worker normally accustom to crafting fine bows for his majesty's men. As the centuries passed, golf equipment design and construction fell to blacksmiths, cabinet builders and other such craftsmen. Woods were actually made of wood and irons of iron. It was often a skill passed down from generation to generation but remained relatively part-time work for these men. Some of the early artisans with equipment that survives today include Brits Hugh Philp, Robert Condie and Willie Park. Early golf professionals were also clubmakers. Clubs of the day were painstakingly hand made works of art and commanded a pretty penny then as now.

Shafts around the turn of the century were all wooden made of hickory or ash. Some were made of bamboo. Wood shafts were the norm until the middle of the 1920s when the first steel shafts began to appear. The "Brassie," "Mashie" and "Niblick" were replaced by the 2-wood, 5-iron and 9-iron respectively. Advanced manufacturing processes were churning out clubs by the hundreds as the demand increased.

Early golf balls were called "Featheries" and that's because they were tanned leather pouches filled with feathers. These were particularly misbehaving spheres in the wet weather. The feathery gave way to the "Gutties" or "Gutta Percha" that was made from the sap of the Percha tree. To the dismay of the Gutty makers, American Coburn Haskell discovered that a bunch of rubber bands stretched together to form a circle could be covered and made a much more responsive projectile. The Haskell ball sent the gutty the way of the feathery. Technological advancements made in materials saw the golf ball evolve into the multi-layer marvels on the market today.

The Basics

The three groups of golf equipment—the tools with which the ball is struck—are woods, irons and putters. The material references can be misleading to the novice because today most woods are made of metal, there is not an ounce of iron in most irons and putters can be made of wood.

Each of these pieces of gear is constructed mainly the same way. The shaft is connected to the clubhead at a point called the hosel. The grip fits over the shaft at its top end and is where the hands connect with the golf club. Various glues and tapes are used to bind these parts together.

All three of these main parts work as one to allow the golfer to swing the club efficiently enough to make contact with the ball on a consistent basis. The important thing to keep in mind is that no combination of shaft, clubhead and grip is going to hit the ball on its own. As the saying goes, "It's the indian, not the arrows." However, not all equipment works for all swings. A general knowledge of how these parts work together and separately will make it easier to choose a set that functions best for each individual's golf swing.

Shafts

Many top professionals still prefer steel shafts in their irons and woods because they believe steel is more consistent. Graphite shafts are very popular but also more expensive. Some shafts are made of titanium or other combination of metals.

Flex and kickpoint are two shaft buzzwords. Shaft flex refers to the extent a shaft bends during the takeaway and downswing. A stiff flexed shaft bends less than a soft flexed version. Kickpoint is the area of the shaft the does most of the bending. A shaft with a low kickpoint bends more toward the clubhead end while a high kickpoint shaft does most of its bending toward the grip end.

Shafts also twist, bow, torque and vibrate. It's most important—and this will be a recurring theme throughout this equipment section—to see a professional and try a few shafts before buying a set of clubs or re-shafting the current set.

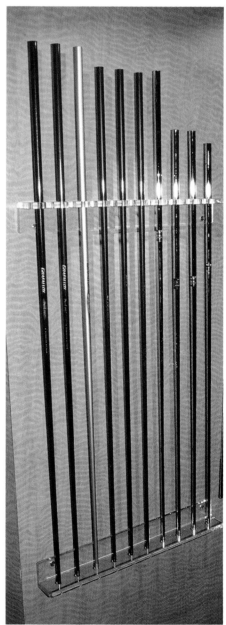

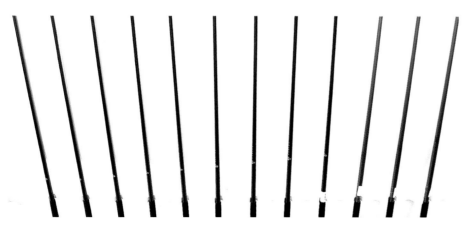

Clubheads

The most important part of the clubhead is the face or clubface. The center of the clubface is what you hope will strike the ball. The area of the clubface farthest from the golfer is the toe. The area of the clubface closest to the golfer is the heel. Most golfers strike the ball with these areas. The bottom of the clubface is the edge or leading edge. This is the portion of the clubhead used for alignment.

To combat the swing faults of everyday hackers, manufacturers produce perimeter-weighted clubheads. These oversized technological marvels distribute the weight of the clubhead evenly around the edge of the face. The idea is to minimize the negative effects of off-center hits.

Early incarnations of the modern iron were called blades. The weight of blades is concentrated behind the center of the clubface or "sweetspot." The majority of Tour professionals still use blades because they are generally considered more easily workable.

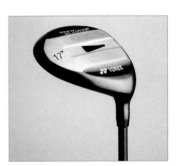

Grips

Few golfers recognize the importance of grips in the overall club makeup. Simply put, they are your only connection to the golf club. Executing a proper grip—the physical act of holding onto the club—is the first step toward building a solid swing. It's difficult to execute a good grip if the actual grips on you clubs are not comfortable.

Grips can be made of leather or multiple combinations of rubber and other synthetic materials. Traditional grips were wrapped leather and still exist today. More common are the slip-on type rubber versions with various tacky patterns to facilitate feel. Styles include buffed, brushed, cord and raised. Grips can be thin or thick. Some golfers with big hands prefer oversized grips. Some golfers believe they obtain better feel with thinner grips. The advice is to hit several shots with different types of grips to discover what feels best for you.

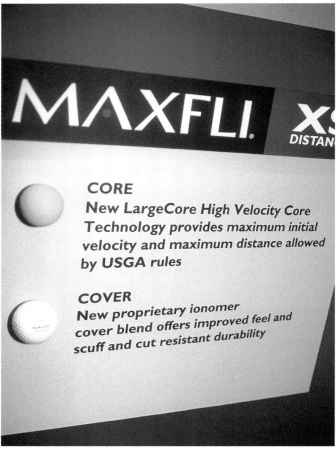

CORE
New LargeCore High Velocity Core Technology provides maximum initial velocity and maximum distance allowed by USGA rules

COVER
New proprietary ionomer cover blend offers improved feel and scuff and cut resistant durability

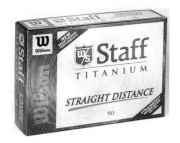

Balls

As stated earlier, ball design has progressed at an amazing rate. Balls that cost $50 per dozen reflect the price of this technology not to mention the marketing dollars spent to convince consumers that one ball is superior to another.

The two things everyday golfers need concern themselves with are spin and distance. Balls fall into these two categories. Those with harder, more durable covers are normally considered distance balls and are designed to fly farther. Distance balls traditionally are constructed of two pieces: a rubber core and the cover. Softer-covered balls are usually spin balls meaning the golfer should be able to shape ballflight more pronouncedly and stop them on the green more easily. Many spin balls are of three-piece construction with a rubber core, wound rubber bands and a balata cover. Today there are hybrid spin/distance balls made of four pieces that include a liquid core. Try a few different ball types, check your funds and play what feels good on course and on your wallet.

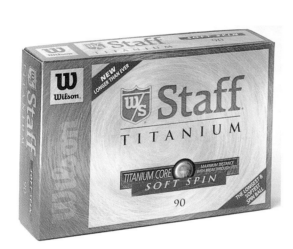

What Clubs to Play

You have a multitude of choices about what gear to carry. Before 1938, some pros carried up to 25 clubs. Then the USGA limited the number to fourteen. The standard make up of a set of golf clubs are three woods, nine irons, a putter and an extra utility club. Normally this club would be a specialty, for example a higher lofted wedge or an extra trouble wood for tough lies.

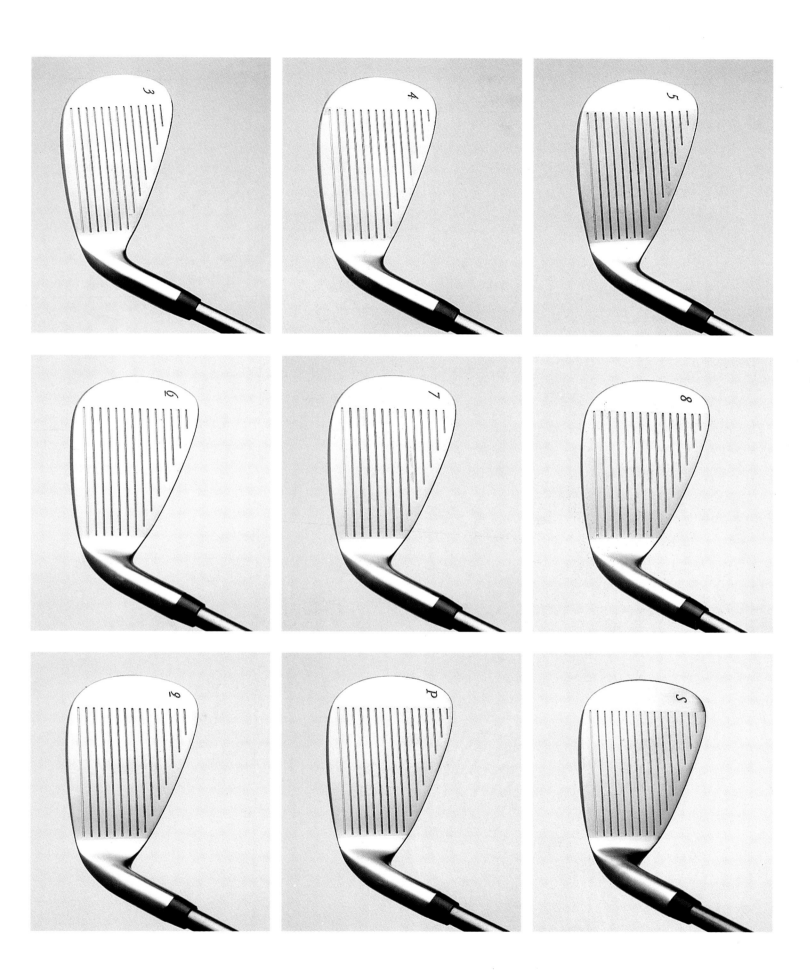

Long Irons or Woods

The advancements achieved in fairway wood design have made them incredibly easy to hit and given golfers an incredible advantage in distance shots from tough lies. Long irons are not easy to hit and tend to get snarled in long grass. The only real advantage to using a long iron is its ability to work the ball more easily than the woods.

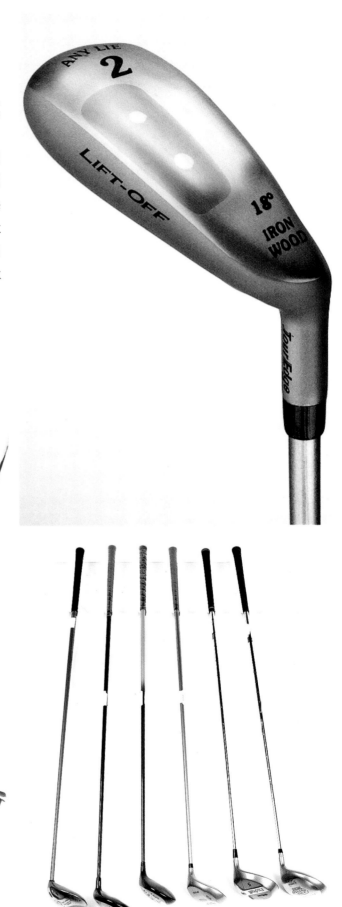

The Driver

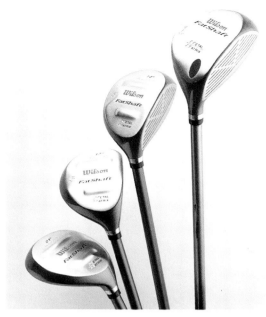

Two things are important when it comes to driving—distance and accuracy. A higher-lofted driver will minimize sidespin and, therefore, hooks and slices. This will compensate for whatever distance you may lose from the ball traveling on a higher trajectory. Beware the temptation to go to a long-shafted model. They are harder to control and require you to alter your swing.

Putters

The type of putter you choose should feel comfortable with the type of stroke you employ. Putters connected to the shaft at the middle of the clubhead are called center shafted and work best for those who employ a straight-back, straight-through putting technique. Heel-shafted putters promote a slight rotation of the clubhead on the backswing and throughswing. With putters, above all other pieces of equipment, it is important you experiment with various types of mallets, blades or heel-toe-weighted models.

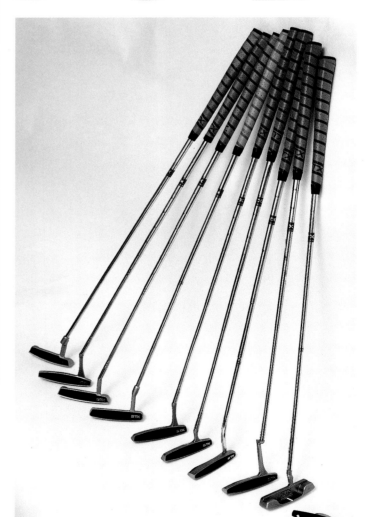

Wedges

It is common to see a Tour professional carrying three wedges and sometimes four. The multiple wedge approach gives good players and players with limited ability more options around the green. Lob wedges (lofts of more than 60 degrees) are excellent tools for delicate green-side shots. Approach wedges or gap wedges allow players to take a full swing from distances in between a pitching wedge and a sand wedge rather than having to finesse one or the other.

Equipment Maintenance

Golf equipment is expensive. A single driver can cost $500 and a premium set of irons runs well into four figures. It pays to take care of your gear not just financially, but well-maintained equipment will allow you to play your best. Here are some tips that will extend the life of your clubs and improve your ballstriking.

Carry a Towel

Grass, mud and water will damage your clubheads if left to dry and cake. A handy towel allows you to wipe your clubheads after each shot. Metal will rust despite marketing claims to the contrary. Dirt in the grooves of your clubface will negatively effect ballflight. Towel off your grips to maximize their tackiness.

Clean Your Grips

Leather and synthetics will wear out much more quickly if you allow sweat and grime to build up on them. After every round, scrub your grips with soap and water and then dry them thoroughly. Replace worn out grips: it's inexpensive.

Get Them Checked

The damage inflicted on clubheads and shafts from the violent collisions with the ball, the earth or any other solid object will alter the loft and lie of your clubs and stress your shafts. Have a professional measure your clubhead's properties and check the integrity of your shafts yearly.

Custom Fitting

On the PGA Tour, equipment manufacturers bring entire trucks filled with machinery designed to tweak, grind and replace parts of its professional's gear. And this is gear built specifically for that professional in the first place. The reason is that top players recognize the benefit of playing clubs with detailed specifications that allow them to maximize their ballstriking based upon their individual swing characteristics. While no truck is going to follow you around, the same basic benefit is available for the everyday player.

Many top equipment manufacturers have some sort of custom-fitting program that allows you to order a set of clubs designed for your swing. You don't have to buy off the rack. Professional fitters will watch you swing, evaluate your tendencies and adjust lofts, lies, shaft lengths, etc., to suit your game. Independent custom-fitters or nearly any club professional can give you the same service. If you've already laid out a lot of money on new clubs, you can take them to a custom fitter to have the specs adjusted. While this service will cost you a few bucks, it's not possible for manufacturers to make one set of clubs that fits every golfer.

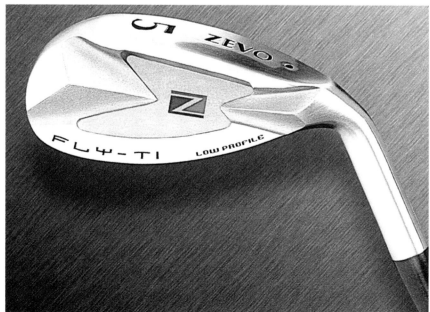

The ACCESSORIES

INTRODUCTION

Chances are some caddies may take exception to being called a golf accessory. Indeed, Tour professionals consider their very well paid caddies a golf necessity. But for purposes of this section, anything not directly involved in club striking ball will be considered an accessory. And there are thousands of them that fuel a billion-dollar marketplace. A few of the more common appear below.

Apparel

For many, it's as important to look good as it is to play good. Golf clothing, as fashion in general, has always been a trendy affair. The early Scots took their fairway wear very seriously. The men of St. Andrews opted for coats with tails and to dress otherwise was considered bad form. As the 20th Century approached, plus-twos and plus-fours were the rage with long argyle socks and the omnipresent hat or cap. Jimmy Demaret was well known for his flair on course opting for bright and occasionally his tam o' shanter. The painful plaids and iridescent pastels of the 1960s and 1970s have given way to the more subdued styles of the 1990s unless you count the flashy Swede Jesper Parnevik. Although Demaret's gregarious apparel tradition is carried on today by Payne Stewart who would have been very comfortable in 1910.

Contemporary golf clothing is a very competitive business. The PGA of America's annual merchandise show reserves an entire half of its exhibit space for apparel companies. One of the show's most popular events is the massive golf fashion show complete with hip music, beautiful models and flashy lights. Mainstream apparel companies have recognized the potential of the golf market and made serious inroads into the industry.

Golf-specific shirts and sweaters are now constructed of lightweight, breathable material cut to allow room for the swing. Outerwear has made great strides with space-age materials capable of repelling considerable wind and rain while concurrently whicking away moisture from perspiration. Style and substance drives the industry and that's reflected in the sometimes-shocking price points.

Training Aids

Today's training aids run from the impossibly simple to the extremely complicated to the wonderfully ridiculous. One of the most effective can be found in your garage—the beach ball. A medium-sized beach ball held between the knees provides an excellent feel for how the legs must work throughout the swing. Other more Medieval devices force you to strap into some bondage contraptions that force a proper swing upon you. Then there are aids like the Golf Foot—a giant plastic sole-shaped number that the golfer attaches to his front shoe. The idea is to keep the front foot grounded throughout the swing. This short review is not to suggest that all of these training aids don't function perfectly well in their intended purpose. It's simply to illustrate the endless range of practice devices available.

There are a couple of things to consider when selecting a training aid. The first is cost. If you're going to spend hundreds of dollars on a practice item, you'll get much more value for your money by taking a series of lessons from a qualified golf professional. The next is effectiveness. Many golf pros warn against aids that restrict your swing or force you into a particular position. Your rhythm and tempo—two extremely important and often overlooked swing aspects—will suffer. They also tend to force you into other bad habits. The best aids serve as a reminder of the swing's proper positions. Find one that addresses whatever flaws you might have and try it.

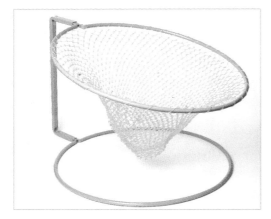

Shoes & Spikes

The advancement made in golf shoe design has outdistanced that of any other non-equipment item. Athletic shoe technology in general has allowed designers to incorporate materials into shoes that boggle the mind. Gel insoles conform to the golfer's foot shape for comfort. Outsoles are extremely water-resistant, durable and supple. Support systems facilitate the motions involved in swinging a golf club as well as walking 18 holes. In short, they're far from the brass-buckled footwear sported by the Honourable Gentlemen of 18th century Scotland.

Spike systems—or more correctly spikeless systems—have been completely revolutionized. Course superintendents have required golfers to wear shoes without spikes to protect fragile green surfaces and improve safety around the non-grassy areas of the club. An entire industry has sprung up that manufacture various replacement nubs, "soft" spikes and the like to take the place of the steel cleat traditionally found on the bottom of golf shoes. Shoe giants like Titleist and Etonic have created whole divisions within their companies stocked with engineers that sketch complicated shoe sole designs that will provide golfers with the traction they need on course while allowing them to walk safely off of it. Subsequently, top line golf shoes have broken the $200 barrier.

Then there is manufacturer Genuin Golf. This European footwear company makes gorgeous golf shoes from exotic materials and fine leathers. If style is your bag, you might consider splurging on a pair of Genuin alligator-skin golf shoes—they'll run you more than $1,400.

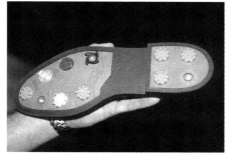

Golf Bags

The massive Tour bags carried on television are not particularly notable except for their size. Really, they're just giant billboards hauled around by the caddie's who soon develop bad backs. But next time you're watching a tournament, notice the criss-crossed carry straps attached to these bags. One of the first to develop this device was Izzo Systems. Their idea was to provide a carry strap that would distribute weight evenly across the back instead of wrenching down one shoulder causing the supporter of such weight to walk with a limp. This is just one of the many innovations built into some of today's high-tech golf bags.

Convenient and poignant pockets of up to a dozen are placed in and around the top bags. They are lightweight and functional. Carry bags feature automatic stands that pop out when you set them on the ground. Some golf bags even have alarms systems built in. There is no end to the modern colors and embroidery available.

The rugged covers and carriers that protect your gear in flight or in the trunk are marvelous in their own right. There is padding in all the right places or hard-shelled cases for the truly tidy. Golf clubs have never been so well guarded.

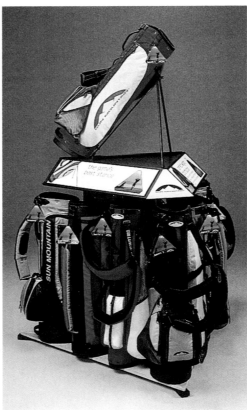

Carts

Traditionalists wince at the use of motorized carts or buggies on the golf course. If you have the opportunity to walk, and feel up to it, have a stretch. But if lugging around 30 pounds of equipment for four miles up and down hills does not appeal to you, there are many options. The pull cart is a popular method among municipal golfers. For a couple of bucks, your clubs can trail behind you. But the true walker who cares not to carry will use one of the new mechanical pull carts that follow the golfer around. You just clip on a transmitter that speaks electronically to the cart. When you walk forward, the cart rolls your clubs forward. When you stop, it stops. It can be a little eerie though.

Private motorized carts or buggies have become quite tricky. Either gas powered or electric, some cart owners have gone to great lengths to soupe up their rides to resemble an expensive Rolls-Royce or rough-and-tumble off-road vehicle. Leather seats and rearview mirrors provide all the comforts of the automobile. Some have lights for night and high-watt radios. If you're going to ride, you might as well ride in style.

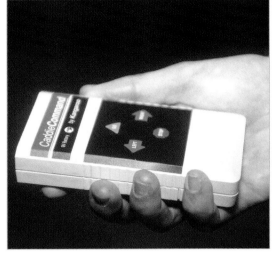

Yardage Devices

It has become imperative for modern golfers to know exactly how far it is to their target. Sprinklers marked with this information do not satisfy everyone. Some golfers now carry yardage finding devices that bounce an infrared beam off of a far away object and measure exactly the distance. These are not legal for tournament play. Expensive courses have installed Global Positioning Satellite devices in each cart that visually displays the distance to a given target as well as provides the opportunity to order drinks from the bar, and be alerted by the club house of any problems.

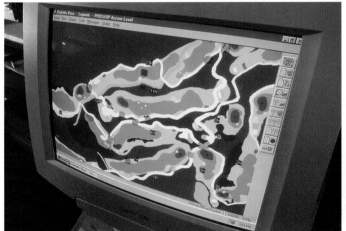

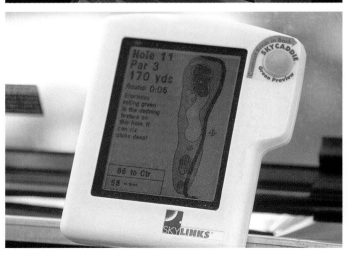
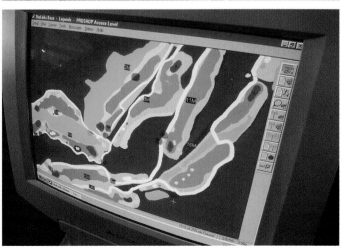

 # Gloves

The cabretta leather tanned to make the top line golf gloves originally came from the South American hairsheep. The thin, durable material gleaned from this hearty animal is perfect for the feel required by good golfers. Scientists have now created synthetic materials that provide nearly the same feel but are much more durable. Manufacturers have also built in mesh sections to provide breathability and additional comfort. Modern gloves are technological marvels.

Tees

In the early days, golfers provided a platform for their tee shots by forming a small sand hill and setting their balls upon it. The only progress made to date is the simple wooden peg that survives today as the tee. The elevation provided by the tee is crucial for the golfer looking to send his ball hurtling down the fairway with the driver. It is recommended however to tee up your ball at any opportunity with whatever club you use off the tee.

Multi-use Tools

The considerate golfer repairs divots made on the green by his golf ball. If you're lucky enough to hit the green, the least you can do is be sure the surface is smooth for the next putter. Divot repair tools are little steel or plastic devices armed with a fork suitable for exactly this task. Many are built with magnetic ball markers and a notched end excellent for cleaning mud from your grooves. Carry one and use it.

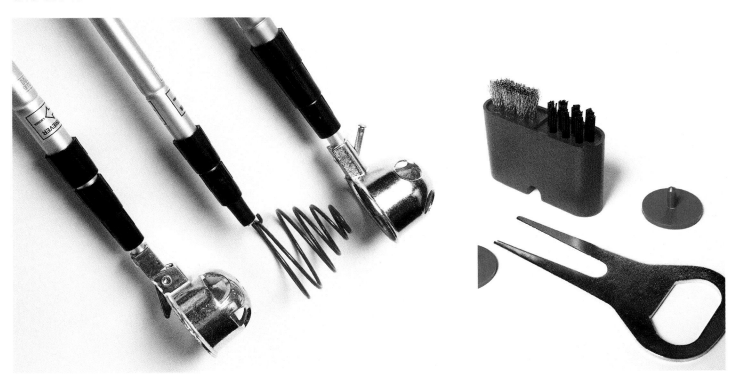

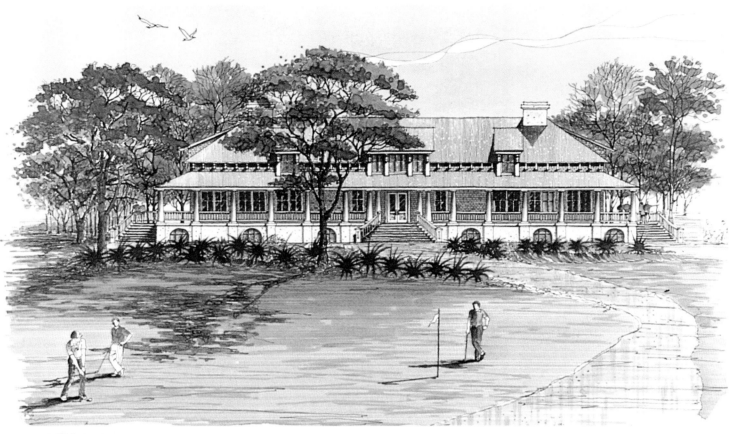

Golf Gifts

The list of golf gift items is endless. Pro shops make as much money from club trinkets and the like as they do from club sales. Buyers can find anything from paintings to collectibles to more useful gifts for the golfer like umbrellas, ball carriers and headcovers.

Golf SCHOOL

INTRODUCTION

Golfers are a self-improving lot. Some take their self-improvement more seriously than others, but everyone wants to get better. And they're all certain they can. You may hit only one or two good shots during your entire round, but the pursuit of more good shots keeps you coming back. Or you may hit 14 of 18 greens in regulation and you're convinced you can get 16. Golf is a game of perfection that can never be perfected. You won't come across a great number of ex-golfers. It seems that anyone who's ever picked up the sticks is hooked for life.

There are various methods for improving your game. If you like you can pick up one of the endless offerings in golf instruction books, magazines, videos, CD-roms or related media. You can plan marathon sessions in front of the tube watching the Golf Channel. You can purchase any of the "miracle" golf clubs or training aids advertised ad nauseum. But if you're serious about playing better golf, you need to be evaluated by a PGA professional.

That said, there is no one way to swing a golf club. There are multitudes of wrong ways, but there is no absolutely right way. Avoid an instructor who tells you otherwise. A good instructor is one that will work with what you have. If someone tells you he or she intends to overhaul your entire swing, grab your bag and run. A good golf teacher will ask you questions before they start giving

instructions. A good golf teacher makes you feel comfortable and is aware of your goals. Not everyone is aiming to be a scratch player, some simply want to shave a few strokes off their handicap. A good teacher will approach each individual differently.

Evidence of golf swing differences is on display each week at any professional tournament. Atop the leader board, you'll find many excellent players shooting well under par and not one of them swings the golf club exactly like any of the others. Some PGA Tour players have what is often referred to as a classic swing, Steve Elkington's being a prime example. Others compete with extremely unorthodox motions: Jim Furyk's has been compared to falling out of a lawn chair. The differences can be due to physical make-up. Short, stocky players like Craig Stadler and Ian Woosnam employ a flatter swing plane. Taller players like Tom Weiskopf and Bob Charles attack the ball from a much steeper angle.

Differences can stem from habits developed long ago. Fuzzy Zoeller sets up with the ball planted near the neck of his irons; not many instruction texts will recommend such a position. The South African Bobby Locke employed an extremely shut address position and hit superlative hooks (he even applied draw to his putts). A lot of top players simply have varying philosophies on the golf swing.

The Professionals

Peter
Hymes

Richard
Shoemaker

Jennifer
Buchanan

Mel
Sole

Tim
Jackson

Tom
Planker

Some top touring professionals are extremely meticulous about their golf swings. No one has delved as deeply and successfully into the fundamental mechanics of the golf swing as the great Ben Hogan. But more and more of today's golfers treat the study of the golf swing as a matter of scientific research. Tom Kite, Nick Faldo, Gary Player and Colin Montgomerie are all great students of the golf swing. Others, while still paying attention to mechanics, play the game more by feel. Lee Trevino, Seve Ballesteros, Ben Crenshaw and Tom Watson are tremendous feel players.

The point is you don't have to be a disciple of *Hogan's Five Lessons: The Modern Fundamentals of Golf* to enjoy the game, although it is one of the classic texts. But there are some undeniable basics to striking the ball well, and those will be presented in the following pages.

The experts even argue about some of the basics. Alternative approaches to various swing aspects are also available. You will find more detailed explanations of methods for escaping trouble, shaping shots and getting your ball in the hole once you've reached the green. All of the advice presented is intended to serve as a blueprint for you to develop and refine to suit your individual style. It is intended to help you get better.

BUILDING BLOCKS

Be careful of the temptation to employ some of the more advanced sections of the instruction before mastering the all-important points made regarding grip, stance and alignment. While these sections are not the most exciting, they are undeniably crucial to continuing along your path to better golf. It requires a fairly advanced understanding of your swing to make adjustments during your stroke. Even with an acute understanding, such adjustments are not recommended. The beginner golfer, however, can make adjustments in grip and setup that will go a long way to improving the overall swing. A mastery of the basics is forever reliable. If things begin to go awry on the course, you can scale back to the basics and hopefully get it righted again. If you don't master the basics, you will continue to flail away.

It has been said that the golf swing should be taught as one fluid motion. Thinking of it as such is helpful in developing critical tempo, timing and balance. But it is actually the combination of and connections between the individual components within the larger motion that allows you to create the flowing stroke. Don't believe for one second that the powerful, seemingly effortless swings of the world's top golfers are not rooted in the very fundamentals

mentioned above. No less of an authority than Nick Faldo has admitted he probably tinkers with and refines his grip and setup more than any other aspect of his envied swing. These fundamentals must be mastered before you can hope to get better.

DO THE TIME

Chances are that you've played golf with the same flaws for many years. Your body has ingrained improper motions. Your muscles, joints and tendons are used to flowing and firing in familiar ways that may or may not be technically sound. For this reason, integrating new, correct movements into your golf swing will at first feel very awkward. It will feel wrong. You will be uncomfortable and probably spray shots all over the practice range. Don't get discouraged and do be persistent. Incorporating proper fundamentals into your swing is the only way to develop a repeating, solid stroke that will minimize mistakes and serve you well on the course. Eventually the proper movements will become more familiar and you will begin striking the ball more consistently. It is during this phase that it is most beneficial to work with a professional. He or she can monitor your improvements and give you the encouragement helpful in working through the changes.

It would be wonderful to be able to provide a set of instructions that would transform you into a single-digit handicapper

overnight. Unfortunately, that is not possible. Improvement will take time. Rest assured that what you're doing will simplify your swing and make it more dependable.

GOLF SCHOOLS

Not everyone has the patience or inclination (or even the cash) to spend a weekly hour one-on-one with their golf professional. Golf, after all, is much more fun to play than to practise. You may prefer to utilize your precious little golf time on course. This is a completely understandable point of view. However, your game is not likely to improve at all, as you will continue to make the same mistakes shot after shot.

An increasingly popular method of gaining instruction is to attend any of the number of golf schools held all over the world. Attendees usually spend mornings in small-group instruction with a PGA professional and afternoons on the course. Some schools offer afternoon rounds with the pro--a unique opportunity to receive practical course-management instruction not normally available. There are golf schools that focus exclusively on the short game, golf schools for left-handed players and golf schools for women only. Individuals are normally grouped into ability levels.

Packages offered at many of the schools include meals, lodging and playing privileges. You'd have to dig into your vacation time

to get to one, some of which last five days or more, but it's a great way to hone your swing and still enjoy your time on course.

Many of the schools videotape your personal instruction and allow you to take home the footage to study on your own. Some even offer a follow up video lesson in which you send back your own tape for critique after you've worked on the lessons learned at the camp. This is a unique and valuable tool.

MORE THAN PHYSICAL

A positive mental outlook is crucial to becoming a good golfer and one with whom other golfers will enjoy spending an afternoon. It's often said that you can learn a lot about a person by playing a round of golf with him. If you tend to get frustrated and upset with poor play on-course, not only are you thought of as a boor but also the chances are that you'll hamper your chances of improving your game. It's difficult enough trying to make swing adjustments while playing. If you're angry or preoccupied with a particular fault, not only will you be unable to correct it but the rest of your game will likely suffer as well. It is important to be physically relaxed and to maintain a sense of humor and humility about golf or you'll just continue to be frustrated and lose focus. In addition, the temperamental golfer is seldom invited to make up a four for a friendly round.

GOOFY FOOTERS

The editors would like to apologize to our left-handed friends. Rest assured that we consider southpaws as important to golf as righties but the complication of explaining all of our instruction text to include both types of golfers would be unmanageable. Please utilize all of the information contained herein—just flip it around. Life would be less complicated if we were all ambidextrous.

Or would it?

SOURCES

There have been published thousands of golf instruction texts. The advice and fundamentals contained in *Golf School* are a combination of styles espoused by some of the greatest, most consistent swingers of a club: Jack Nicklaus, Steve Elkington, Nick Price, Tom Kite and Nick Faldo are just a few. While these men have many differences in terms of physique and in the details of their swings, they all practise many of the fundamentals the same way. No one expects you to swing the club exactly like these great champions, but if you can work with their basic ideas, you can develop a solid stroke of your own.

WARMING UP

INTRODUCTION

Golf isn't as physically demanding as playing basketball. Some people don't even consider golf to be a sport. All of you walking around with sore backs and bum shoulders will heartily disagree. The motions involved in swinging a golf club put a great deal of strain on your spine, your joints and your muscles. There is a lot of force exerted in an unfamiliar fashion. Consequently, you must prepare your body for battle.

Before you embark on any pre-round or pre-practice stretching, walk around for a few minutes to get the blood flowing. You don't have to break into a sweat, although it would help, but it's much safer and more effective to stretch after your muscles are slightly warm.

The exercises explained on the following pages are by no means a complete regimen. They are a simply a few suggestions to help you get ready to play. Performing such exercises will help prevent injury and avoid stiffly hacking around the first few holes. Incorporating a daily stretching routine—not just on golf days—will improve your game and your overall health.

If you're concerned about nagging aches and pains, put down your driver and consult a physician.

Clubs Behind

Lay two clubs across your shoulders.

Slowly rotate your trunk to the right and then to the left. Stretch clubs overhead and then hang.

"As you rotate left and right, you should be in the address position with your lower body. It helps to simulate the motion involved in swinging your club." PH

Hand on Head

Place your left hand against the left side of your head and lean over to the right.

Hold for 30 seconds and switch sides.

Swinging Two Clubs

"Some people use a weighted club for this exercise and that is fine. Just be sure to take it slow and don't over swing—you can hurt yourself." PH

Use two clubs to simulate a slow version of your golf swing.

Concentrate on tempo and be careful not to swing too aggressively.

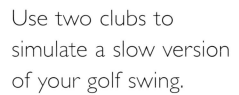

"Try to be aware of the pace of your swings on the range and take that out to the course. This no place to fiddle with your golf swing. Concentrate on pace and go play." MS

Pre-Round Range

Pre-round practice range work should focus on loosening up your golf muscles.

Avoid the temptation to work on swing mechanics.

"If you're pressed for time, hit at least a dozen balls with an iron that you normally hit well. Build some confidence." MS

Pre-Round Putting

Concentrate on tempo before your round.

Develop putting confidence by finishing up with three-holed putts. Don't leave on a miss.

"Take three balls and putt from nearly the same spot every time. You'll get more information on the speed of the greens." TJ

PUTTING

INTRODUCTION

Jack Nicklaus, in his classic instruction book *Golf My Way*, calls putting "that other game." The inference is that green work is completely separate from everything you do to get there. This is frighteningly true. How frustrating it is when it takes you more strokes to roll the ball 20 feet than it did to fly it 365 yards from tee to green! For this and many other reasons, putting is as mental an exercise as it is physical.

Good stroke mechanics will help you to become a solid putter—and variations of these are presented in the following pages. But it is an attitude of confidence and fearlessness that defines the truly great putters. Arnold Palmer and, in his major-winning years, Tom Watson would fairly ram the ball into the back of the hole; such a method succeeds only if you have the courage born of total confidence in both your putting stroke and your ability to "read" the greens.

When your putting is on, you can shave bunches of strokes off what might otherwise be a mediocre round. When you're putting poorly, you can destroy a solid ball-striking day. Putting can be depressing and exhilarating, unforgiving and surprising— but it's never boring.

The beginner golfer may never be able to manufacture an intentional draw with his 4-iron, but with enough practice he can expect to get down in two from 35 feet. Sometimes the hole looks big—and sometimes you wonder if it's there at all.

Regular Putting Grip

Rest the shaft gently across the bottom pads of your left hand. Place your right hand below.

Overlap your left forefinger on top of your right hand.

"There is no absolute way to hold your putter. It really is a matter of personal preference. You'll be a better putter if you're comfortable holding the club." TP

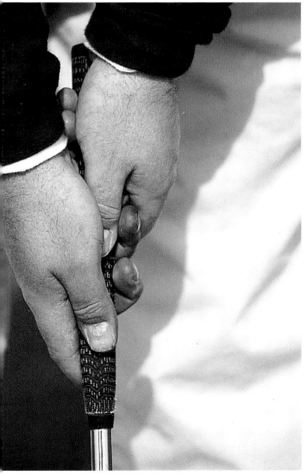

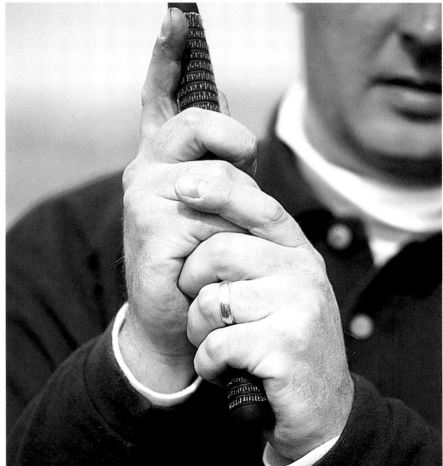

Left Hand Low/Cross

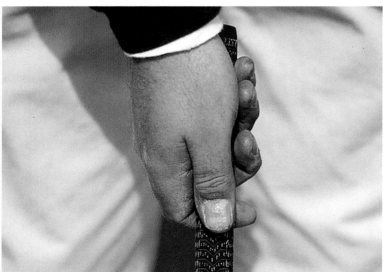

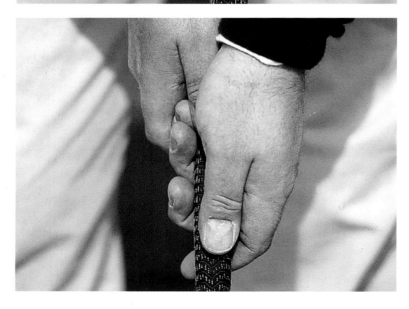

Some golfers reverse their hands placing their left hand below their right.

The idea is to take your wrists completely out of the stroke.

"This putting grip forces your right hand to remain solid and continue on down the line of your putt. It also helps your wrists to remain firm." TJ

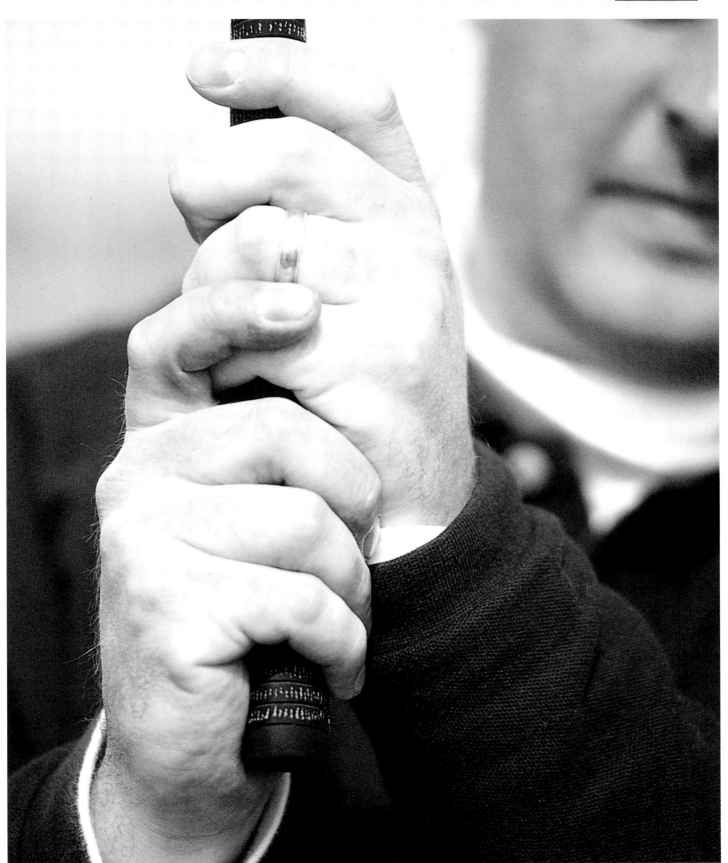

Stance & Alignment

Play the ball in the middle of your stance with your knees slightly flexed.

Your eyes should be directly over the ball.

"A thin piece of white tape or chalk placed on the top edge of your putter can help you to be sure your putter face is square to your target line." TJ

PRO TIP

"Break your putts into three sections. Read the first third, the second third and the last third." RS

Green Reading

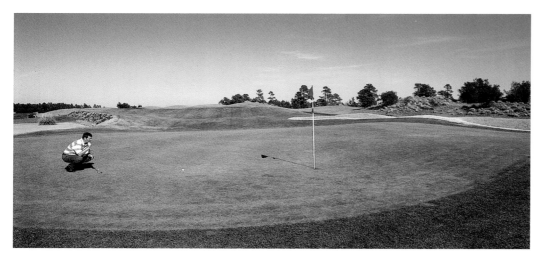

Begin reading the slope as you approach the green to determine drainage and overall pitch.

Squat about three feet behind your ball.

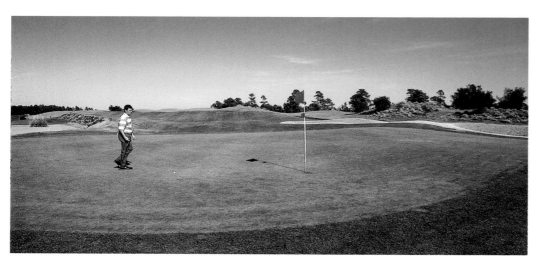

"Most amateurs don't pay enough attention to the direction of the grain. When you get to the green, take the time to check the way the grass is growing. Your putts will move faster down grain and slower against the grain." TJ

Read the break from behind your ball then walk around to the other side of the pin continually judging the slope.

Squat opposite your ball and read again.

"Treat all putts as straight putts." TJ

Plumb Bobbing

This tricky technique involves squatting behind your ball while holding your putter about mid-shaft.

Extend your arm out straight with your club straight up.

"You must determine which of your eyes is dominant. Focus on an object and then close one eye. If the object moves then your closed eye is dominant. That's the one you plumb bob with." RS

With your ball between your club and the hole, notice how much the green slopes relative to your shaft.

Move to the opposite side and repeat.

"Plumb bobbing is a very difficult exercise to master. I recommend amateurs practice the technique exhaustively before they try in on course otherwise they're only likely to slow up play." MS

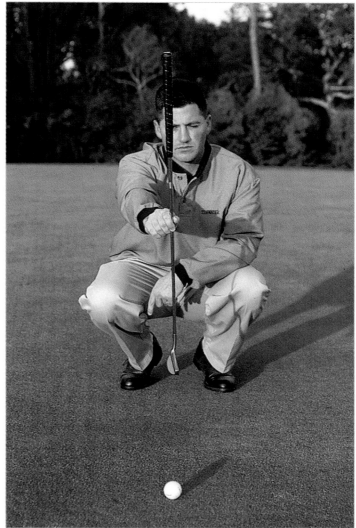

The Putting Stroke

You must be relaxed over your ball. Many golfers take a deep breath and exhale on the takeaway.

"Focus on keeping your head still, you'll hit the ball solid just about every time." TJ

The most important aspect is good tempo.

Bring the clubhead straight back or slightly inside and return it through the ball on exactly the same path.

"Many folks who are not putting well can trace the problem to a breakdown in the wrists. Their wrists are bending and they're not using enough of their shoulders." TP

Be confident.

Long Putter Stroke

Hold the long putter with your left hand high and your right hand low to create a straight back/straight through pendulum motion.

"The upright stance of the long putter can be more comfortable for golfers with bad backs. It also takes the wrists completely out of the stroke." TJ

Lag Putting

While you want to make every putt, it's critical to get your ball close with the first attempt.

"Most amateurs will leave long putts short. Focus on getting your ball at least a foot past the hole. Good long putting requires a lot of practice as well." TP

Three-putting is demoralizing.

Missing Amateur Side

When you leave a breaking putt below the hole it's referred to as "missing on the amateur side."

Most golfers never read enough break.

"When you leave a putt above the hole it's referred to as 'missing on the pro side.' The reason is that professionals are more likely to read too much break." TJ

Putting Drills

Putting only with your left arm forces you to concentrate on controlling your stroke on a steady path.

"Putting with just one arm also encourages you to keep your body very still. If you don't, you're going to have a tough time hitting the ball solidly." TJ

It also helps to discourage the use of wrists and hands in the putting motion.

Place a tee at the point where your putt breaks and putt only to the tee.

PRO TIP

"Putting to a tee on a breaking putt will also make you better at reading greens. You'll develop a more thorough understanding of how slopes affect roll." TJ

This drill helps you hone distance control skills.

Lay two clubs behind your putterhead parallel to each other.

"Most poor putters will bring the clubhead outside the line and cut it coming through. This drill encourages overspin as opposed to sidespin." TJ

This "railroad track" helps you visualize the straight back/straight through path.

Place three balls equidistant from the hole on four sides.

"This clock drill is excellent for building putting confidence. You really get to know the feeling and visualization of the ball going in the hole." TJ

You must make all three at each station before you move on to the next.

FULL SWING GRIPS

INTRODUCTION

It's been said countless times in golf instruction: your hands are your only connection to the club. The point is obvious but extremely important and often overlooked. Your grip determines absolutely everything else that happens in your golf swing. A poor grip eliminates virtually any chance you have of executing a decent stroke. You may not be able to feel where your clubhead is at the top or the point where your shaft flexes, but you can feel that club in your hands. It is one of those fundamentals that is impossible to overstress: develop a good grip.

What is a good grip? There are three grips taught by golf instructors: the overlapping or Vardon grip, the interlocking grip and the less popular 10-finger or baseball grip. Whichever you choose, a good grip is one that's comfortable. It's one that you can repeat consistently. A good grip allows your hands to work together, not against each other.

Grip pressure is just as important as how and where you place your hands on the club. Choking the grip adds stress to your entire swing. A tight grip leads to tight forearms, which leads to tight shoulders on so on. Don't kill your swing before you even take the club away from the ball.

GOLF SCHOOL

"You want to be able to see two knuckles on your left hand." PH

Grip

The Vardon grip involves placing your right pinkie on top of your left index finger. The interlocking grip crosses these two fingers.

The baseball grip has all 10 fingers on the club.

"Your hands need to work together as one unit." PH

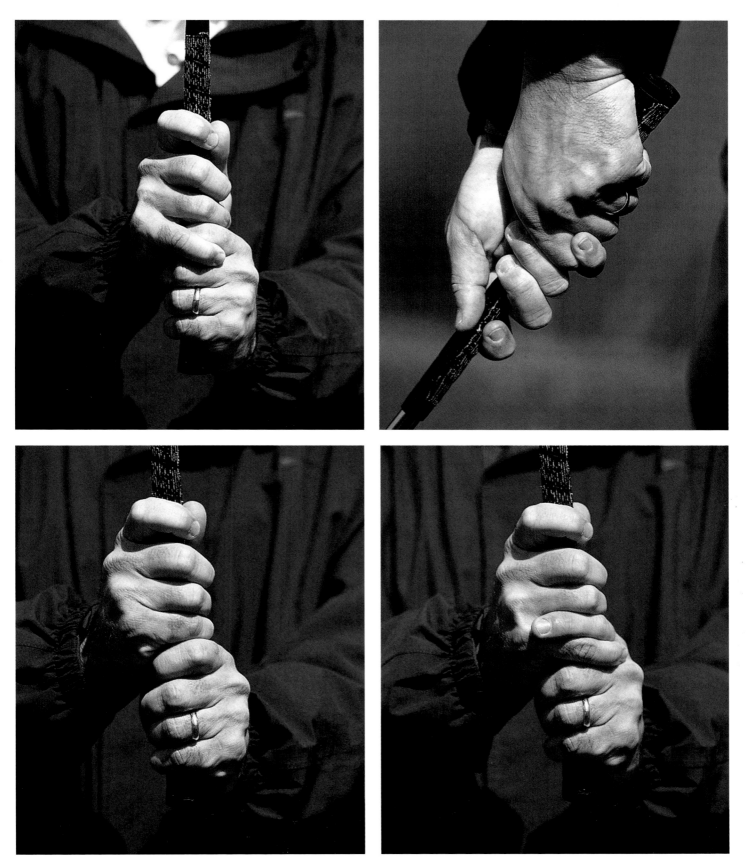

Grip Pressure

You must grip your club firmly enough to maintain control yet softly enough to avoid unnecessary tension in your hands, arms and shoulders.

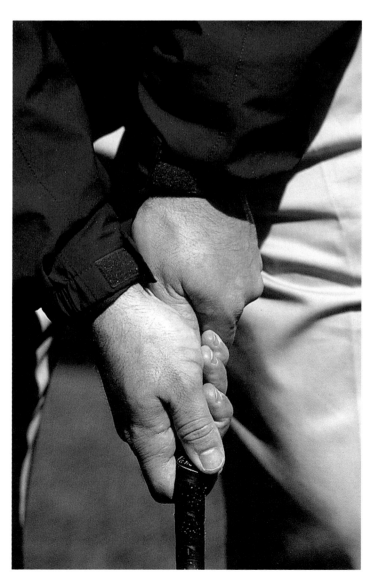

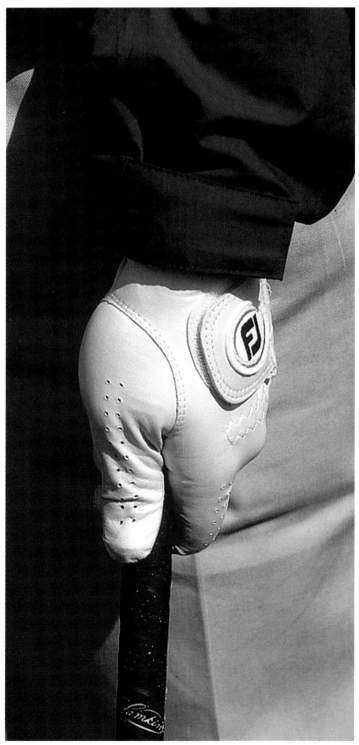

"If you can feel your forearms flex you're holding the club too tight." PH

PRO TIP

GOLF SCHOOL

Grip Strengthening

Plunge your right hand into a bucket
of sand and extend then flex your
fingers 10 times.

Repeat with your left hand.

PRO TIP

"It's important to have strength in your hands because it allows you to control the club more effectively. You're not looking to choke the club, but a firm handle is desirable." MS

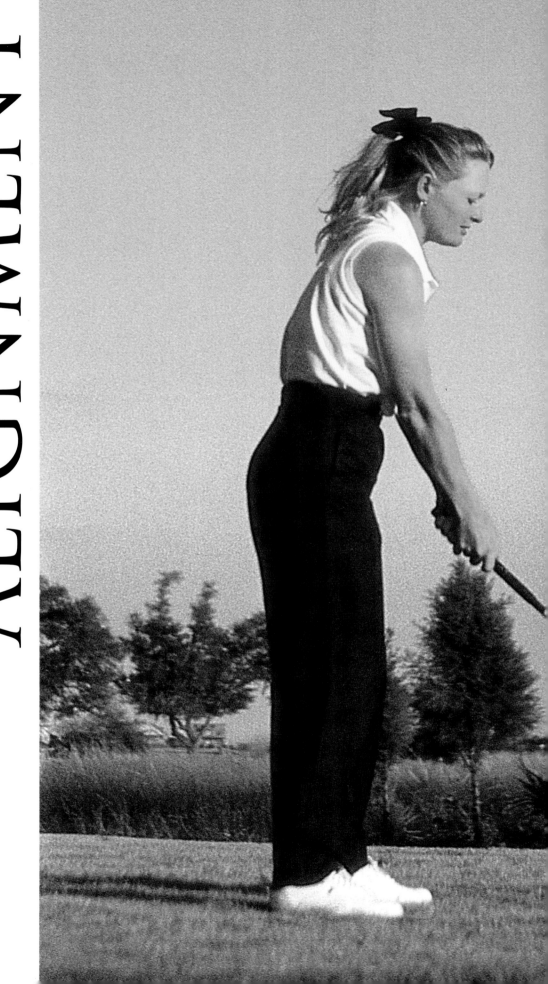

SET UP, STANCE, ALIGNMENT

INTRODUCTION

There are several decisions to be made before you set up to the ball. Among other things, you must choose the target on which you wish to land your ball; you must choose the right club for the distance to that target; and you must assess the lie you're faced with. All of these choices effect how you'll eventually set up to the ball.

The physical aspects of set up, stance and alignment—also referred to as the address position—will be explained later in this chapter, but the overriding theme again is comfort. A stable, balanced and comfortable position is the only one in which you have any prospect of striking the ball solidly and consistently. A well-struck ball accomplished from a faulty set up position is a stroke of luck. The address is where you establish the base on which the rest of the swing depends. If your address position is not dependable, your swing will be unstable.

Set up, stance and alignment elicit possibly the least amount of controversy within the golf-instruction community. Most agree there are few variables in a good address position. It needs to become second nature.

Spine Tilt/Knee Flex

Relax over the ball with your knees slightly bent and your arms hanging straight down from your shoulders.

"Many amateurs set up to the ball in a close fashion because they're sure they're going to slice it. A closed stance will actually increase the chances of hitting a slice." RS

Bend from your waist.

Rotation / Balance

"If your spine angle moves throughout your swing you are actually changing your distance from the ball. It's nearly impossible to return the clubface squarely to the ball if you've altered your distance from it." MS

Your stance should be solid enough that a person would be unable to push you over from front or back.

Your spine angle must remain constant.

Address Illustrations

Your forearms should be even. Your clubhead's leading edge should be square to your target line.

This position gives you the best chance to hit the ball consistently.

"I set my clubhead behind the ball before I step into the stance to ensure it's pointed at my target." RS

Waggle & Relaxation

Many golfers wiggle their feet or waggle the club to release tension.

Check the your intended line of flight to ensure proper alignment.

"There needs to be a certain amount of motion over the ball. Too many amateurs are absolutely static at address and they can't possibly make a smooth swing from there." MS

TAKE AWAY

INTRODUCTION

You may think it unnecessary to focus an entire chapter on the takeaway, but the swing's first several inches are from where the rest of your backswing grows. Mess up this part of your stroke and the only way you'll get the club back on line is to manipulate it in some unnatural way. This is a recipe for disaster.

The takeaway provides one of the most frequently used swing keys: "low and slow." A fuller explanation of this key appears later but the fact that it is rooted in the takeaway suggests just how important this part of your swing is. Not only do you set the shape and timing of your backswing here: if you do it correctly, you also establish the tempo for the remainder of your swing.

Just where the pre-swing ends and the takeaway begins is a matter of debate. Golfers initiate their swing with differing amounts of motion. But the takeaway should not be started from a static position. The golf swing is an athletic motion. A certain amount of movement is expected prior to taking the club back. If you don't employ a waggle, or wiggle your feet slightly, or some such motion, you're likely to have too much tension in your body.

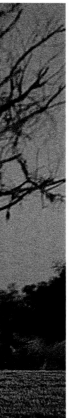

The Take Away

The first few inches you take the club back should be directly along your target line.

The movement is made with your arms, shoulders and hands as one piece.

"Don't let the clubhead get behind you too quickly." MS

Take Away Drill

Practice on the range with two clubs in a "railroad track" formation behind your ball.

"The takeaway is a motion made primarily with your shoulders. Golfers get in trouble right off by manipulating the club back with their hands." MS

Many golfers tend to yank the club inside immediately on the backswing.

BACKSWING

INTRODUCTION

The backswing is perhaps the most important part of your golf swing. This is where you generate your power and begin the crucial transition to the downswing. The backswing is where your weight begins to shift, your wrists break and you start to turn around your body. This is where the golf swing truly becomes an athletic movement. This is where coordination takes over. Not surprisingly, this is where the better golfers start to distinguish themselves from the hackers.

Backswing technique varies from golfer to golfer. Mostly this depends on physical makeup. You may get the club back flatter or steeper depending on your size and range of motion. The important thing is to establish a plane for the remainder of your swing and to stick with it. It is dangerous to think of manipulating the club onto a specific plane. Your backswing should feel natural, not contrived. The only way you'll be able to get the club moving back toward the ball with any consistency is if you take it back similarly. The aim is to replicate, on your downswing, the trajectory of the clubhead back, up and around your body on the backswing

You're fighting gravity on the backswing and the sensation is strange. But remember, you're really only storing energy.

PRO TIP

"Don't be afraid to let your wrists cock fully. Your arms and body work together as a unit" JB

Backswing

As the club continues back your wrists begin to hinge and your upper body should rotate against the slight turn of your hips.

"Most amateur golfers take the club too far back. When you go too far back you're out of balance and you have to make adjustments to get back to the ball." TP

"Allow your shoulders to turn fully." MS

At the top nearly all of your weight should be on your back leg in an athletic and comfortably positioned coil.

"Take the club back only to where you think it's three-quarters full. This will probably put you exactly where you need to be." TP

DOWNSWING

INTRODUCTION

The downswing, also called the forward swing, is your opportunity to let gravity work for you. It's important to think in terms of unwinding and riding gravity because this helps prevent you from yanking the club from the top. The downswing begins as your club ceases to go backward and starts to come forward toward the ball—also known as the transition. The transition is the point where your club feels the least controllable. It's not a comfortable position, but it is not one to be feared. You must be confident that through your set up, your takeaway and your backswing, you've given yourself every opportunity to return the clubhead back to the ball with the proper motion. If you've done everything correctly up to this point, the rest should be easy. Of course, it's not.

Earlier it was stated that many feel the golf swing should be taught as one fluid motion. Nowhere is this truer than in the downswing. Focusing on the return of the clubhead back to the ball can produce some scary results. If you allow it to happen naturally, while being aware of the proper mechanics, you'll have a much higher chance of success.

The Downswing

Your transition down should be slow and controlled.

"Try to pull the club down with your left arm and hand. That's not to say you should yank the club from the top because that results in a casting of the clubhead. Just go slow." TP

Unwind your upper body on an inside to out swing path to the ball.

Your weight transitions to your left side as you strike the ball.

"Don't complicate things." TP

Contact the ball as your club is still descending. The divot comes after impact

FOLLOW THROUGH

INTRODUCTION

The elation you feel for finally having struck the golf ball often restricts the last phase of your swing—the follow through. You've set it up, you've taken the club back steadily, you've dropped it into the slot and then you slow the clubhead down just before impact only to produce a powerless slap at the ball. If you don't complete your follow through that's exactly what you're doing, restricting the speed of the clubhead through the ball. Don't make this mistake. A complete swing includes a full, balanced finish.

A less-than-complete finish will not only sap power from your stroke: it usually causes you to pull your head and thus your body, which greatly reduces your chance of hitting the ball squarely. This is another power sapper and normally will cause the ball to be hit off-line. An incomplete follow through is also an indication that there exists an element of tension during the whole swing. In addition, not following through is often a result of poor balance.

The Follow Through

At impact your head and your spine still should be behind the ball. As your hands drop through the hitting zone, their momentum pulls your upper body along.

"Concentrate on taking your clubhead through the ball and three inches past it before you turn your head. This helps you keep the club on line through the hitting zone." TP

"When you're in full finish, your belt buckle should be facing your target." TP

Allow your arms to continue up and around your shoulders.

"A balanced finish position is one in which you're not falling forward or backward but posed proudly on your front foot." JB

Nearly all of your weight will be on your left leg with your chest facing the target.

TIMING, TEMPO, RHYTHM

INTRODUCTION

As you've been told, golf is an athletic movement. The swing requires strength, flexibility and a certain amount of grace. It's not enough to master the mechanics of grip, set up, backswing, and downswing, etc. You must be able to mold all these steps into a smooth, well-choreographed movement. This is done with timing, tempo and balance. A mechanically sound golfer without these elements in his stroke is not hard to spot. He's the robotic-looking fellow.

To develop a sound swing, it is necessary to break it down into its basic parts. Then, as suggested, you must master these parts before you can hope to put them all together. But in all the practice and drills you employ, you must always maintain a sense of timing, tempo and rhythm. The pre-shot routine has its own rhythm; there is a critical element of tempo in the take-away, etc. Timing, tempo and rhythm are what allow you to put it all together.

Timing, Tempo, Rhythm

A good golf swing resembles a ballet movement. Good golfers make their strokes look effortless.

They do this with superior tempo and rhythm.

"Timing makes distance." TP

PRO TIP

"Timing is the key to the whole golf swing." TP

Timing, Tempo, Rhythm

"The biggest problem many golfers have is trying to hit the ball too hard. This usually means they take the club back too far and then try to kill it. Itís impossible to have good timing in this situation." TP

Take the same amount of time in your backswing as you do in the forward swing. This notion also helps you build consistency.

PRE-SHOT ROUTINE

INTRODUCTION

The routine you perform before starting the clubhead back is important for you both mentally and physically. A good pre-shot routine, as explained in the next few pages, allows you to aim properly, relax your mind and set up to your ball with the best chance of hitting a solid shot.

There are countless ways to prepare to hit your ball. The important thing about a pre-shot routine is that you develop one and follow it to the letter every time. You can have a simple, quickie routine or a complicated, drawn-out saga of a routine. Often a golfer's pre-shot routine corresponds to his overall mental outlook. A feel-type golfer tends to get through the set quickly. The more thoughtful golfer may labor through the choreography.

A pre-shot routine begins from behind the ball. This is the only place you have the opportunity to view your target and line of flight with an undistorted eye. That's why the pre-shot routine is so important to aim and alignment. The greatest asset of a well-rehearsed pre-shot routine is the opportunity it provides for you to settle down, calm your nerves and take a deep breath. It is here you eliminate all fears and develop confidence.

Pre-Shot Routine

"When aligning yourself from behind the ball, pick out an interme-diate target that you can easily spot from over the ball." JB

A repeatable pre-shot routine allows you to set the tone for a repeatable swing. Develop a tempo and sequence for action before your swing and carry that over.

"See the ball flying through the air from behind to impress it in your mind." MS

Pre-Shot Routine

"You should have a pre-shot routine for your full swing and a separate routine for your short game and putting. Use them every time." MS

Normally your routine will involve some visualization from behind your ball and continue until you take the club away.

CHIPPING

INTRODUCTION

A good chipping day can often compensate for a less-than-stellar ball-striking outing. Weekend golfers may not hit a ton of greens in regulation, but those who can get up and down from near the green will still score well. You can get yourself out of a lot of trouble with a good short game. Chipping is an especially enjoyable part of the game for the imaginative player because it provides the best opportunity to create shots with the least amount of risk. You can chip with a variety of clubs depending on your lie and path to the hole. The stroke itself is really little more than a putting stroke made with anything from a sand wedge to a 5-iron. One technique explained later even shows you how and when to chip with your 3-wood.

The weekend player often overlooks this part of the game. You may consider it more fun to bang driver after driver down the practice range, but you are wasting your time. Chipping is one area every golfer can improve and it may be the easiest to improve because of the uncomplicated motions involved. It is also the area of your game that will most positively effect your score.

303

"Your hands and your head are set behind the ball and should remain there throughout the entire stroke. Your hands go back low and finish low." TJ

Set Up/Swing

"Your goal is to keep the ball down and get it rolling quickly. It's an extension of a putt." TJ

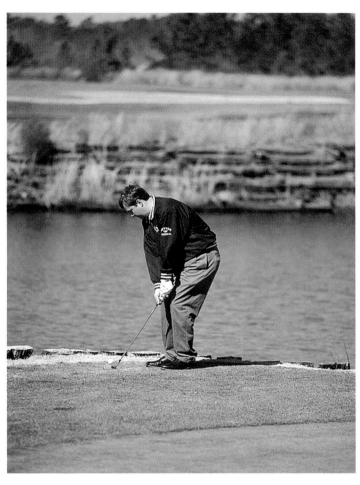

With your feet practically together, open up your stance relative to your target line.

Play the ball off your back foot.

"The lower you can fly your ball the more likely it is to remain on line. Expect to make it." TJ

Choke down on the grip. Make a smooth stroke incorporating little wrist break.

Do not decelerate through impact. Rhythm is the key.

Chip & Run

If it's possible for you to keep your ball near the ground take advantage of this. Use a 6-iron or 7-iron and take a normal chipping stance.

"Chipping is basically a long extended putting stroke." TJ

Hit your shot as you would a putt. The decreased loft of a mid-iron will allow the ball to roll upon landing. This high-percentage shot can save you.

"You can use just about any club in your bag for this shot. You need to take your bag out to the practice green and get a feel for the different distances." TJ

From Rough/Bellied

Heavy rough around the green can make it difficult to execute a normal chip. One option is to strike the ball with your wedge's leading edge.

"Set the back of your wedge on top of the rough and treat the shot like a putt. You eliminate the possibility of snagging the club on the takeaway. Make a good follow through." TJ

Three-Wood Chip

Choke down on your 3-wood and take a normal chipping stance.

"The large soleplate on the wood will literally flatten the grass as it comes to the ball as opposed to an iron that may snag in the grass." MS

Make a putting stroke and let the wood run the ball to the hole.

Chipping Drill

The long shaft on this practice club helps ingrain the feeling of keeping your wrists steady through impact. Loose wrists increase the margin for error.

"This drill forces you to keep the clubhead on line. When the hands are too involved, the clubhead tends to get manipulated inside or outside and that results in mis-hits." JB

PITCHING

INTRODUCTION

The difficulty of pitching should not be underestimated. Pitching is tough because there are so many variables to consider. For example, do you want to hit a pitch shot that stops immediately next to the hole? The answer is: only if you must.
(In any case, few high-handicap players can put the right amount of backspin on the ball to stop it dead on landing.) Do you want to pitch the ball halfway and let it run up to the hole? Only if you can. Pitching is an exercise in decision making and then mechanics.

Pitching is also difficult because so many pitch shots require less than full swings. Any time you must manipulate the length of your swing you increase the chance of doing something wrong. You'll get the mechanics of pitching later. For now, focus on your decision making.

The basic idea is to keep your ball as close to the ground as possible. It's much easier to determine what your ball will do if it's rolling. The axiom has always been: if you can't putt it, chip it. If you can't chip it, run it to the hole (the "bump-and-run" shot widely used on Scottish links). If you can't run it, then and only then fly it to the hole. It's always romantic to consider yourself a wedge wizard, but the smart player only lofts the ball when it's necessary—if, for instance, he has to hit the ball over an obstruction such as a bunker or pond.

Pitching Swing

The absolute key to solid pitching is rhythm.

No matter if you're attempting a half-, three-quarter- or full-pitch shot, concentrate on swinging smoothly with equal tempo.

"Control the entire shot with your body and not necessarily with your arms."-MS

Punch Low/Spinner

Play the ball back in your stance and make just a three-quarter swing.

Think of trapping the ball and restrict your follow through.

"Get the ball on the ground as soon as you can. Then it can follow like a putt. The more you try to fly the ball to the flag the more likely you are to make an error." TP

Flop Shot

This shot is useful when you must carry the ball to the hole and land it softly. Play the ball back in your stance and choke down.

"Don't chicken out coming back through." TP

"The harder you hit this shot the higher the ball is going to go." TP

"Have the guts to hit it. Don't stop, because you're going to chili dip it if you do." TP

Lay your clubface wide open. Think of swishing the clubhead right under your ball. Concentrate on rhythm and commit to the shot.

Soft & Lofted

A high lofted pitch from the fairway is one of golf's most difficult situations.

"Concentrate on hitting the back of the ball first. Don't take a lot of turf with it. You want to just pick it off the turf." TP

Open your body and the clubface and try to clip the ball off the turf.

Low Spinner

This miniature punch shot allows you to stop your ball quickly.

"If you must fly it, focus on a spot on the green where you want to land the ball. Too many golfers just focus on the pin."-TP

Close down your clubface and smother the ball into the turf.

SAND PLAY

INTRODUCTION

Men like Gary Player and Seve Ballesteros are famous for their uncanny ability to extract the ball from the greenside bunker and deposit it near or in the hole. Many Tour players would rather play from a bunker than longish rough nearby. The lesson is that greenside bunkers are not as difficult as most amateur players' fears make them out to be. Most leisure golfers never bother to learn the proper technique of escape.

Fairway bunkers are a different story. Course designers include fairway bunkers on their courses to penalize a wayward shot. And they will penalize. There are several factors involved that make fairway bunkers extremely difficult. First you must overcome the mental anguish of just having hit your ball so off line that it ended up there in the first place. Then you must negotiate whatever lip might exist and gauge the distance required for a ball not sitting on grass.

In the next few pages you'll learn how to increase your odds of getting greenside bunker shots close and how to survive bunkers out in the fairway.

Set up/Swing

For a greenside blast, open your body to the target line and play the ball back in your stance.

"An open stance will help you get your body through the ball." RS

Choke down on the club.

Focus on a spot one inch behind your ball. Swing along your shoulder line and strike that spot.

"Make sure your clubface points at your target." PH

The club will propel sand and your ball high and softly.

Firm Wet Sand

The bounce built into your sand wedge requires you clip the ball from this situation rather than attempting a normal blast.

"It's crucial to strike the sand firmly behind the ball—do not hit it thin." TJ

Up Slope in Sand

Set your shoulders at the same angle as the slope.

Choke down and make an aggressive stroke and bury the clubhead into the slope just below your ball.

PRO TIP

"Treat your wedge as a shovel to just get it out. Use some extra grip pressure because you'll be chopping down pretty violently." TJ

Down Slope in Sand

"Keep most of your weight on the low side. Focus on staying down through the ball." PH

Set your shoulders at the same angle as the slope. Follow the slope's angle back and through, working to strike the ball first

Long Blast

The greenside blast technique can be utilized from farther away with lower lofted clubs.

Be sure you use a club with enough loft to clear any lip.

"*Be sure you choke down enough on your club relative to how much you dig your feet in the sand.*" TJ

"Take one to two clubs more than you normally would from that yardage." PH

Fairway Bunker

"Prayer helps." PH

The key swing thought here is to strike the ball first. The more sand you take, the less likely you'll enjoy good results. Keep your body quiet and swing smoothly.

Fairway Wood Bunker

"Keep your lower body quiet to avoid spinning out of the shot. Focus on striking the lower half of the ball first." PH

Not a shot for the faint of heart, you first must decide if the risk may outweigh the reward.

It's critical to swing smoothly and clip the ball from the sand

Sand Practice

Bury a short board so that the sand just covers it.

"Beginners find this drill ideal for gauging just how much sand is needed to get the ball out of the greenside bunker. They become familiar with the proper peeling motion and develop confidence." JB

Practice your splash technique to get a feeling for the bounce involved.

"As the ball buries further under the sand, the golfer learns it will come out with less spin and roll more once on the green. They must take that into consideration and attempt to land it accordingly." JB.

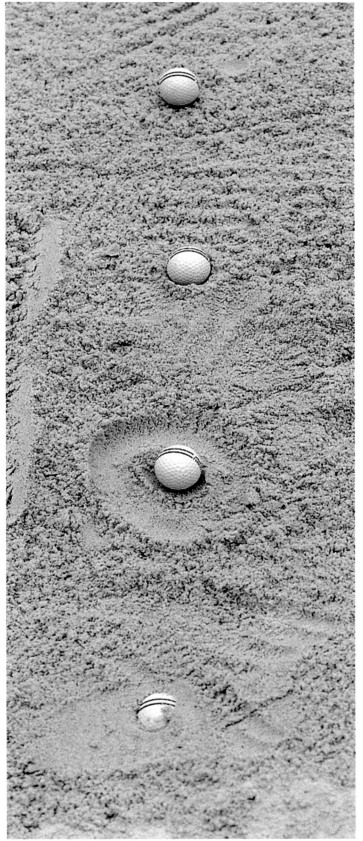

Bury four balls in progressively difficult lies.

Hit the exposed ball first. You'll need to take more sand as the balls sit farther down.

IRON PLAY

INTRODUCTION

Most golfers feel reasonably comfortable operating with their short and middle irons—the 9-iron through 5-iron. Chances are your favorite club is one of these because they are commonly the easiest to hit the ball with. The reason is that the shafts are shorter than the long irons and woods, you stand nearer the ball and you're more comfortable hitting down on the ball, which is the proper way to strike it. You have less inclination to "help" the ball into the air because you trust the higher lofts built into the short and middle irons.

Your accuracy with the short and middle irons allows you to get the ball nearer the hole and produce lower scores. So it is important to know what distances you can obtain from each of these clubs. Spend some time on a well-marked practice range—even this method is difficult—and gauge how far each of your irons flies. Normally, you should expect about a 10-yard distance gap between a full shot with each one.

Once on the course, be careful to gauge accurately the distance to the hole. You must decipher where the pin is cut on the green, wind conditions and lie. Once you're comfortable you've got the right distance and have selected the right club, swing with confidence. You know you can hit it.

Full Iron

Play the short irons with your ball nearer the front of your stance.

PRO TIP

"No matter what iron you're using, it's important to focus on making a full shoulder turn. This helps you maximize your distance potential and increases the likelihood you will finish with a full follow through." JB

The middle irons are played with the ball in the center of your stance.

Long Iron

The long irons are played with the ball slightly back in your stance.

"People think they have to hit long irons hard—you don't. Just let the club do the work." TP

Don't be intimidated by the decreased loft. Strike the ball first and swing smoothly.

Fade

Set the clubface directly on the line you want the ball to start.

Open your stance relative to that line and swing along your shoulders.

"Many people will try and hit this shot too hard and end up double-crossing themselves. Instead of cutting the ball the face remains closed and you pull it." TP

Fade

"Focus on an area where you want your ball to start turning. Obviously you want the ball to turn to the pin, but you want to focus on the target where it's going to turn." TP

The ball will start along the line and your outside-to-in swing path will cause the ball to move from left to right.

Draw

Set the clubface directly on the line you want the ball to start.

Close your stance relative to that line and swing along your shoulders.

"Focus taking the club away on a definite inside path. This is the best method to get the club to come back from the inside resulting in the right-to-left ball flight." TP

The ball will start along the line and your inside-to-out swing path will cause the ball to move from right to left.

"Another technique for drawing the ball is to align your feet on the line you want the ball to start and point your clubface at the target. It's the same idea." TP

Knock Down

Play the ball in the middle of your stance and set your hands forward.

"Your wrists need to remain firm all the way through the ball. Try to keep that clubface along the target line as long after impact as possible." TP

Take a smooth three-quarter swing and keep your hands low through impact.

High Ball

Play the ball forward and take one club extra. Choke down and concentrate on sliding the club under the ball.

"Think about catching the ball on the upswing. Stay down through the shot but focus on impact after the bottom of your swing arc." TP

Finish with your hands high.

Creating Spin

Play the ball slightly forward and choke down on the grip.

"Concentrate on hitting through the ball. This will help ensure that you contact the ball on the way down and don't catch it thin by pulling up through the ball. Don't take too steep an angle to the ball." PH

You must strike the ball first and accelerate through impact.

WOOD PLAY

INTRODUCTION

The importance placed on huge drives is comical. The galleries that assemble for Tour big hitters John Daly, Tiger Woods and Davis Love, among others, are massive because everyone likes to see these guys launch their tee shots. And it is indeed impressive to watch the ball fly far down the fairway and tumble 300 yards away. But you'll notice that these players are not achieving their distance by trying to hit their drives hard (well, maybe Daly does). Their distance is achieved by swinging smoothly, with excellent tempo and precise balance.

Amateur golfers are too preoccupied with distance at the expense of accuracy. The driver is a difficult club to hit. The shaft is long, there is less loft on the face and your swing is bigger. All of these elements combine to reduce your chances of striking the ball properly. When your mental state is to kill the ball to achieve maximum distance, you're sure to increase the odds even further. Once you've made the decision to use a driver off the tee— and this should not be an automatic decision—remind yourself that this should be the calmest-swung club in your bag.

Driving

"The pace of your driver swing should be the same as your irons. Many high-handicappers feel they have to kill the driver and they swing too fast." MS

Play the ball forward in your stance and widen your feet. Think about striking the ball on the upswing. Swing smoothly.

"Most amateurs use too stiff a shaft in their driver and often their driver shafts are too long." MS

Rhythm is paramount with the driver.

Avoid the temptation to swing hard and focus on a gentle transition.

"Be sure to get full extension with your arms all the way through the shot." JB

Fairway Wood

"Don't try to lift the ball with your fairway wood." JB

Utilize these heavier clubheads to create precise tempo. Strike the ball first and allow the face's loft to propel your ball upward and onward.

Driving Iron

The smart golfer moves down to an iron off the tee when faced with a tight landing area. Sacrifice distance for accuracy.

"A lot of amateurs fail to get their weight to the left side on the downswing which creates a slice." TJ

TROUBLE PLAY

INTRODUCTION

How pleasant golf would be if every ball sat proudly up on the fairway, invitingly ready to be struck. As you know, more often than not the ball huddles dourly in some sort of less-than ideal spot, daring you to hack it out. The lie of the ball dictates how you must attack it. Most of the instruction thus far has been directed toward strokes made at a ball sitting in the fairway or light rough. Now you'll learn what to do in circumstances that test your technique more severely.

How often have you wondered to yourself, "Is there an even lie anywhere on this damn course?" Balls lying uphill, downhill and sidehill are some of the most tricky to deal with. Equally as frustrating are balls in a divot, balls in heavy rough, balls on bare spots, etc. All these and more are covered in the following pages. There are also sugges-tions for thoughtful course management and for club selection depending on your lie. Learning how to execute the trouble shots is vital if you are to make them less troublesome.

Uphill Lie

Play the ball forward in your stance with your shoulders set along the angle of the slope.

"The ball will move in the air in response to the severity of your lie." MS

Take one more club than the shot calls for.

Downhill Lie

Play the ball back in your stance and lean with the hill.

"If you concentrate on keeping your weight more toward your back foot you will better be able to maintain your balance on this difficult shot." TP

Take one less club because the ball will run. Strike the ball first.

Ball Above Your Feet

Choke down on your club and take one more than normal.

"Take a practice swing from the slope to find the bottom of your swing arc." JB

Stand a bit erect and swing on a flattish plane. Be prepared for the ball to move right to left.

Ball Below Your Feet

Concentrate on balance and utilize exaggerated knee and hip flex.

Swing smoothly and be prepared for the ball to move left to right.

"The balance, particularly on your follow through is crucial." JB

"Play the ball back in your stance and hit the ball first." TJ

Heavy Rough

"You need to have a firm grip on the club. Once your club gets snarled in the thick rough it has a tendency to turn. Take a nice firm stance when you're in pine needles because your feet are likely to slip and slide around during your swing." TJ

Depending on the severity of your lie, heavy rough tends to wrap around your clubhead and close the face. Aim to the right and strike the ball first.

Shallow Water

"Treat the water shot much like a greenside bunker shot. If the ball is more than one inch under water than you have very little chance of getting it out." MS

Assuming you can actually get to your ball, the trick to playing this shot is in your mindset. You must ignore the fact that you're going to get wet. Accelerate through the shot.

"Play the ball as far back in your stance as possible to give yourself the maximum room to swing through the ball." TJ

Tree Shots

"Choose a path out of the woods that puts you safely back in the fairway—don't try to hit a career shot." TJ

Creativity comes to the fore when negotiating these terrible lies. Whether bouncing off the trunk or flipping around left-handed, concentrate on smoothness.

"In the rain, I'll squat a little more in my stance to feel like I'm really grounded and firm." RS

Rain Play

"Always take an extra club so you can choke down and swing smoothly while still getting enough distance. You won't swing as hard if you know you have more club in your hands." TJ

As uncomfortable as rain play can be, the most important aspect of surviving the water is to impact the ball first. Any shot hit fat is impossible.

MENTAL GAME

INTRODUCTION

You already know how mental putting can be. An excitable fellow will have an impossible time on the greens. The same is true for your play on the rest of the course: the way your mind works effects how your body responds. If you become irate at hitting a bad shot, your chances of hitting the next shot well are extremely slim. There are dozens of books published on nothing but the mental side of golf. Tour players have coaches designated for nothing else other than to help them deal with the psychological torture a high-pressure competitive round can inflict.

Your attitude toward everyday life has a lot to do with how you react on the golf course. If you speed through traffic like a maniac, chances are you have a fast golf swing and have broken a few clubs in your day. Chances also are good that you have trouble enjoying your golf game. Remember that the game is fun and every time you have the opportunity to spend a morning or afternoon on the course is less time you have to spend working. So, don't make work out of your golf game.

Golf is not life and death, it's much more than that —seriously, though, it's just a game.

Mental Game

One of the things that separates the elite players from the good players is their ability to keep it together mentally on the course.

Realize that you're playing golf for fun. No matter what you score remember it's not a train smash.

It's tough enough to swing with tempo and efficiency in the calmest situations. Anger only compounds the likelihood of poor golf shots.

Be realistic in your expectations

Never give up. You're going to get in some trouble on the golf course but you always have the opportunity to make it up.

Only take one swing thought out on the course with you. Don't try to remember everything you've ever learned about golf.

It's much easier to talk about taking one shot at a time but it is very important to maintaining control.

Stay in your comfort zone. For example, don't hit a driver off the fairway if you feel you can't execute it.

There's nothing you can do about your last shot. Make *this* one good.

Not only will your game suffer with frustration, your playing partners will become agitated with your outward expressions of anger.

There's always an option.

Putting is the ultimate mental exercise. You must be confident that you'll make your putts and see your ball going in the hole.

A ROUND WITH THE PRO

INTRODUCTION

♟ *The Pro*

♟ *The Novice*

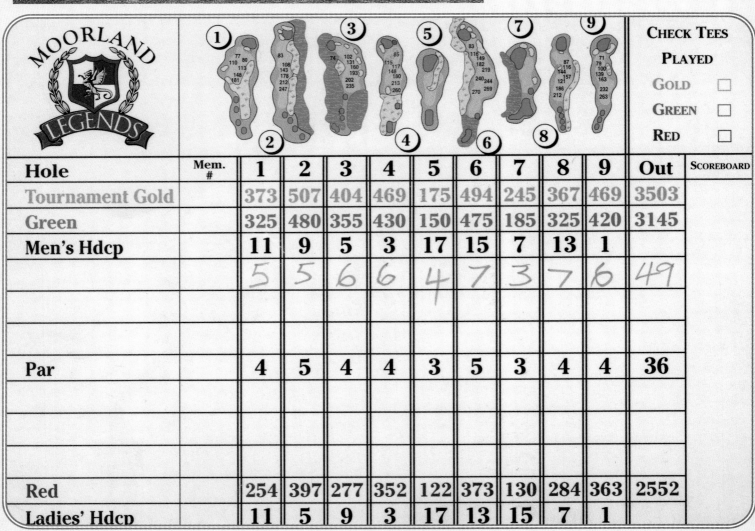

MOORLAND LEGENDS

CHECK TEES PLAYED

GOLD ☐
GREEN ☐
RED ☐

Hole	Mem. #	1	2	3	4	5	6	7	8	9	Out	SCOREBOARD
Tournament Gold		373	507	404	469	175	494	245	367	469	3503	
Green		325	480	355	430	150	475	185	325	420	3145	
Men's Hdcp		11	9	5	3	17	15	7	13	1		
		5	5	6	6	4	7	3	7	6	49	
Par		4	5	4	4	3	5	3	4	4	36	
Red		254	397	277	352	122	373	130	284	363	2552	
Ladies' Hdcp		11	5	9	3	17	13	15	7	1		

Course Ratings / Slope

Tournament Gold	73.1 / 128
Green	69.8 / 121
Red	72.8 / 118

STEPHEN SOVETTS
Head Professional

The Legends • Hwy. 501 • P.O. Box 2038 • Myrtle Beach, S.C. 29578
800-552-2660   803-236-9318

Date: _____

Scorer: _____

Attest: _____

In 1991, the Legends facility opened the second of three courses—Moorland—to extremely positive reviews. Architect P.B. Dye's rolling and rollicking design earned high marks in several leading publications' new course listings. Many feel the target layout is one of the East Coast's most difficult.

Golfers are forced to execute cunning and daring shots from tee to green on nearly every hole. The course's devilish bunkering and penalizing employment of vast waste areas will challenge even the most experienced players. While severe at times, the course's stunning natural terrain and possibility for reward provide an extremely enjoyable round for both accomplished golfers and those of lesser ability.

The following pages detail Moorland's 18 delightful holes. Head professional Tim Jackson takes you around the track providing insight into the course management necessary to score well.

Accompanying Tim is our fearless publisher, Suneel Jaitly—a high-handicapper possessing great enthusiasm and a John Dalyesque backswing. Suneel takes you around the course while attempting to heed Tim's advice.

As a form of torture, Tim was forced to play his ball from wherever Suneel ended up. Rest assured Tim found himself in areas of Moorland that he never knew existed. The following photographs document their round.

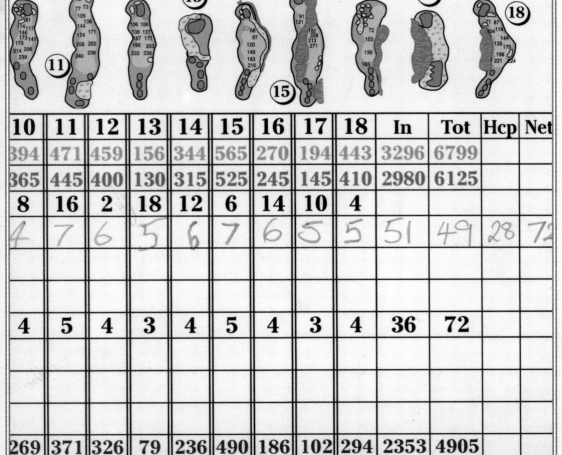

10	11	12	13	14	15	16	17	18	In	Tot	Hcp	Net
394	471	459	156	344	565	270	194	443	3296	6799		
365	445	400	130	315	525	245	145	410	2980	6125		
8	16	2	18	12	6	14	10	4				
4	7	6	5	6	7	6	5	5	51	49	28	72
4	5	4	3	4	5	4	3	4	36	72		
269	371	326	79	236	490	186	102	294	2353	4905		
8	10	2	18	14	4	12	16	6				

Hole One

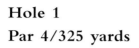

Hole 1
Par 4/325 yards

The short length of this hole allows you to play a fairway wood or long iron from the tee. A large waste bunker running up the right side suggests running your tee ball up the left center of the fairway.

The blind approach is to a shallow green that runs away to the right. A sinister bunker looms short. There's a bailout area left of the green. This is a birdie hole for the good player and can build confidence for the amateur.

Suneel hurts himself right away by swaying too aggressively on his driver takeaway.

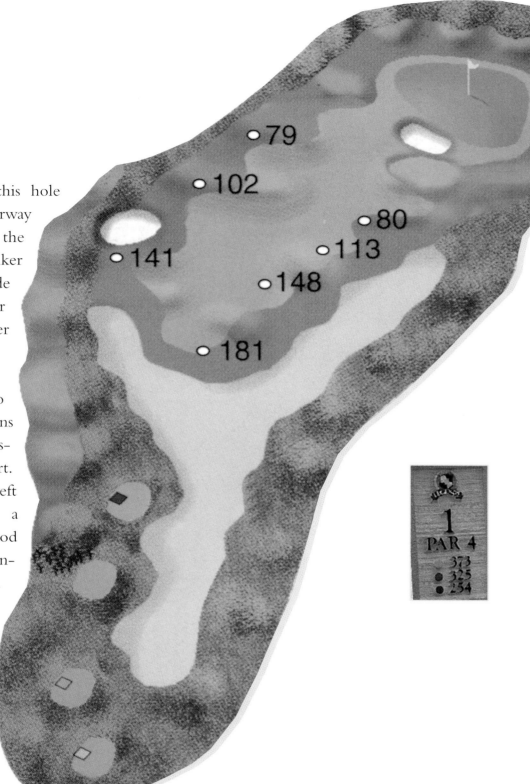

While luckily he found the fairway, we made bogey on a hole where par is very attainable.

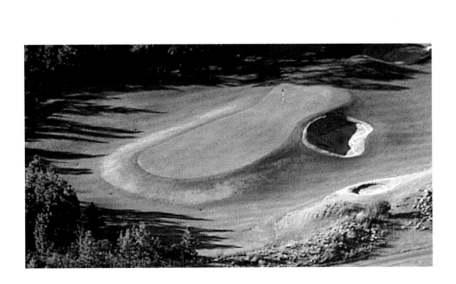

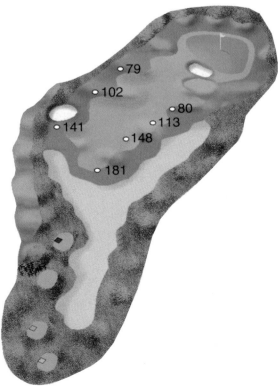

79
102
141
80
113
148
181

G O L F   S C H O O L

Hole Two

You can see Suneel is trying to hit this fairway wood too hard.

Hole 2
Par 5/480 yards

A generous landing area signals driver off the tee. Aim for the left side of the fairway and fade your ball toward the center. Two massive waste areas run along the right side with water lurking right alongside.

Only the foolhardy will attempt to hit the green in two shots. The water wraps around the back of the hole and the green drains directly into it. The smart play is to lay up with a mid-iron leaving a short shot to the green.

A terrific two putt from fifty feet helped us save par much to the delight of our handicapper.

LEGENDS

2
PAR 5
- ○ 507
- ● 480
- ● 397

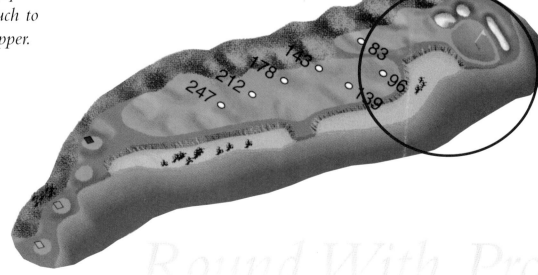

Hole Three

Hole 3
Par 4/355 yards

This time Suneel is able to keep the driver on plane and the result is a useful tee shot.

The tee shot over water is definitely made for a power-fade driver. Be careful not to try and cut off too much of the corner — it's not necessary. There's much more fairway to the right than first apparent.

The approach is also over water to a peninsula green. A bailout area exists right of the green housing two bunkers that see a lot of action. Though it's better hitting from here than splashing in the hazard.

*Unfortunately his approach from a downhill lie found the water
and he had to scramble for double.*

Hole Four

**Hole 4
Par 4/430 yards**

A monstrous par-4, it's the longest at Moorland. This signature hole is home to "Big Bertha," an omi- nous bunker that is better left alone. Aim to the right of her setting up a long approach.

The mounds crossing near the green result in a deceptively blind approach shot. The green appears at least one club nearer than it actually is. Club up one and let it fly. Long will not hurt you.

Our amateur's ball was teed far too low and the result was a topped shot that barely cleared the waste bunker.

Ariel View

From the severe slope, Suneel yanked his ball way left into the woods. This is a hole we were glad to finish.

Hole Five

Hole 5
Par 3/150 yards

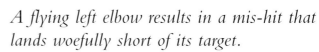

A flying left elbow results in a mis-hit that lands woefully short of its target.

This short par-3 provides menace in its severely sloping green. Sweeping from left to right and slightly forward, the smart player will shoot for the back left of the surface.

The green is also considerably elevated from the tee. A large bunker guards the right side with forest standing behind. If you're going to miss the green, miss it short left.

Second View

Hole Six

Hole 6
Par 5/475 yards

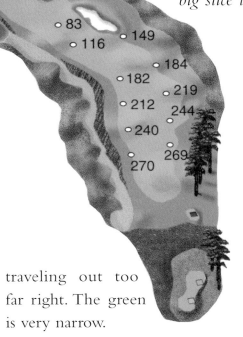

The prudent play here is driver out to the right side of the fairway. Accurate drivers can attempt to blast on down the left but flirting with the waste bunker and gorse crawling there is not a good idea.

Lay up on the right side of the fairway to take the water that surrounds the left side of the green out of play. Avoid the four pot bunkers that welcome shots traveling out too far right. The green is very narrow.

Suneel is unable to advance the ball from this bare lie and it takes four shots to reach the fringe.

Hole Seven

Suneel comes off his shot just slightly but ends up safe. A fantastic bump-and-run results in our second par.

Hole 7
Par 3/185 yards

This long par-3 will test your mettle. Water lurks all along the left side of the hole. If you can manufacture a draw with your club of choice, give it a try. The bailout shot is short right.

The green is an adventure in itself. Characterized by rolling undulations, it slopes from front to back. A shot hit too far left will find the water and two bunkers sit out to the right.

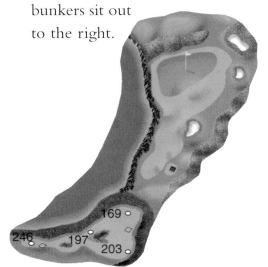

Hole Eight

Drive View

Hole 8
Par 4/325 yards

The short par-4 welcomes a fairway wood or long iron off the tee. Whatever you choose, do not pull it because left is jail. Aim down the right and leave yourself a short iron into the green.

The approach is to the most elevated green on the course. Avoid being short because a penalizing pot bunker waits from which extraction is difficult at best. The green itself is fairly flat.

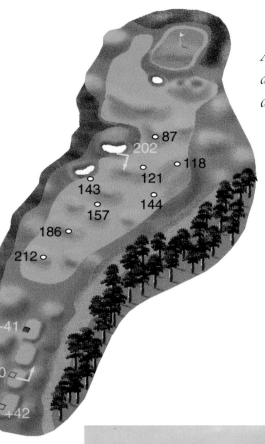

87
202
118
121
143
144
157
186
212
-41
0
+42

A characteristic reverse weight shift causes a weak slap with the driver and reduced distance.

Second View

After a horrendous backswing, Suneel advances the ball just a few yards. A well struck pitch flies the green and we end up with triple.

Hole Nine

Hole 9
Par 4/420 yards

Number nine is a terrific and challenging finishing hole. At 420-yards, it's the number one handicap. The tee shot is a driver aimed directly at Legends' impressive clubhouse, which will leave you in the right center of the fairway.

Too far right will find you in an ugly waste bunker. Assuming you find grass, it will be a long iron or fairway wood into a long green. Take one more club than you think you might need.

79
109
139   163   260
167
197
232

-57
0
+49

Notice how my clubhead stays on plane while Suneel's is obviously coming at the ball from the outside. Second View

His slice puts us in a horrible bunker. Suneel strikes the sand too far behind the ball and barely escapes the hazard.

A decent approach finds the fringe where Suneel deftly bumps to tap-in range. Result: double bogey and 49 for the front.

Hole Ten

Despite a frightening overswing, Suneel makes solid contact and finds the fairway. A good approach and two putts make par.

Drive View

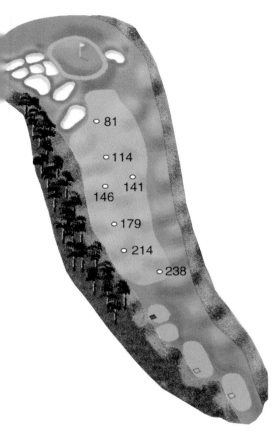

Hole 10
Par 4/365 yards

There's plenty of room for your driver here. Favor the left side of the fairway but beware the forest near the left edge. A giant depression looms on the right edge that falls off the fairway about 20 yards.

The approach is to a three-tiered green that can vary up to three clubs depending on the pin placement. A host of bunkers are assembled on the left side with a lone bunker right.

Second View

Hole Eleven

Suneel again is able to return the clubhead to the ball from his gigantic wind up and ends up in the fairway.

Hole 11
Par 5/445 yards

This is a likely birdie hole for the golfer who can keep the ball in play. The fairway is wider than it looks and invites you to unleash your driver to leave yourself a long-iron second shot. There is no shame, however, in lying up. Most of this hole's trouble is around the green. Miss it left or right and you're likely to end up in one of the deep bunkers set there. Short or long is acceptable. The green is elevated and slopes from front to back.

Second View

*A solid second shot leaves just 100 yards in but, alas, Suneel
sculls his shot over the green into the heavy rough.*

His blast flies over the green again and requires we chip back onto the green. We end up with double bogey.

Hole Twelve

Hole 12
Par 4/400 yards

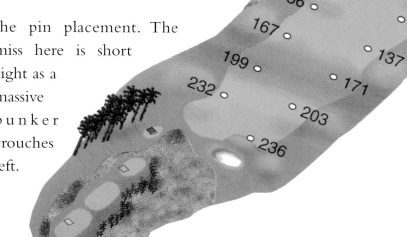

Suneel is able to control his backswing a little more with this drive and is rewarded with a good tee ball.

There is a considerable crown built into this fairway about 200 yards from the tee. If you can carry it, you'll be rewarded with a short approach. If you're short of it, youíll be forced to hit a long uphill shot.

The green is inviting in its size. Don't be fooled. It undulates insidiously so pay attention to the pin placement. The miss here is short right as a massive b u n k e r crouches left.

Hole Thirteen

Hole 13
Par 3/130 yards

From high on this elevated tee
box, this hole looks simple.
The multi-level green
with its queasy swales

77 ○

92 ○

119 ○

145 ○

quickly dashes these hopes. Be certain to check
the direction of the wind before choosing
your club.

A shot short left is deadly. A beautiful yet menacing waster
bunker wraps all the way around the left portion of the green
well below its surface. The bailout area is short right.

*Luck is not with Suneel here as his exaggerated backswing results
in a shot hit on the toe that ends up in the waste bunker short.*

From this spot, I must clip the ball with an open face to get it up quickly. Notice how my hands don't turn over.

77

92

119

145

Hole Fourteen

Suneel fails to get his weight over to the left and hits behind his tee ball.

Hole 14
Par 4/315 yards

68
96
215
120
149
183
216
-79
-20
0
+20
+40

Leave your driver in the bag on this hole. Aside from the wayward tee shot, a drive struck straight and true is likely to find the huge mound running across the fairway at about 250 yards.

The approach is blind so drive up and have look. You will find a slithery waste bunker and forest right and three seemingly benign bunkers left. The green slopes left to right. Short is your best miss.

A chunked chip results in a fringe shot that I choose to execute with my putter as opposed to Suneel who makes the riskier chip shot.

Hole Fifteen

Suneel turns his hips much too far back and can't possibly return squarely to the ball. The shot finds a huge bunker.

Second View

Hole 15
Par 5/525
yards

From the tee, you can be smart and fire a driver at the quad bunkers straight ahead or be fool-hardy and try and find dry land in between those bunkers and the canal on the left. A well-struck shot will easily clear the bunkers. Be smart.

Lay up with a middle iron before the canal comes across the fair-way. Your approach is to a deep green

consisting of three tiers. Note the pin placement because the difference can be two clubs.

The high lip poses a problem for Suneel as he attempts to escape
with too little loft. The ball just ekes out onto the hazard's edge.

Finally we reach the green and Suneel drains a long downhill
putt to finish with a seven on the hole.

Hole Sixteen

Our high handicapper can't resist going for the green with a driver. The predictable result is unfavorable.

Hole 16

Par   4/245

yards

From a distance stand-point this hole is obviously driveable. But they don't call it "Hell's Half Acre" for nothing. Extremely deep bunkers swallow many balls on the left side of this elevated green.

The green is also quite small, which is not good news for those trying to stop a driver. Don't be embar-rassed to play your ball out to the right with a long iron. There's room there and only leaves a short iron to the green.

Suneel attempts this tough chip but sculls it and ends up on the opposite side of the green.

I feel the grass before the fringe is too dodgy to try and roll over so I use a little chip to get close.

Hole Seventeen

An all-arms swing causes Suneel to flail at the ball. Our high-handicapper is suffering from fatigue.

Second View

Hole 17
Par 3/145
yards

A brilliantly constructed tee box—in classic Dye railroad tie-style—presents a true target challenge. Forest all along the left side of the hole is certain death. Long is also trouble. Right is out of bounds.

The green appears as a mirage across a vast area filled with soft sand and vegetation. The surface slopes quickly from back to front. There is no bailout area to speak of unless you're a wizard with your sand wedge.

Hole Eighteen

18
PAR 4
443
410
294

Hole 18
Par 4/410 yards

Avoid any temptation you may feel to shave the corner of this severe dogleg left. Play your ball at the bunker straight ahead and draw it into the center of the fairway. The water and trees on the left are ball magnets.

The green is extremely elevated and a large mound on the right obscures most of it. Two sentry-like pot bunkers secure the front left and right. The green is very large and slopes tremendously from back to front.

A short pitch carries us to the green in three shots. Suneel completes a tough two putt and finishes the back in 51.

And on to the Nineteenth . . .

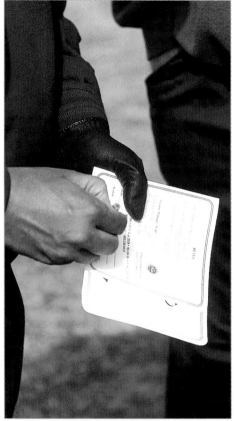

TOM

Tom Plankers has more than 30 years of experience in golf course management. He currently oversees the daily operation of three championship golf courses — Lion's Paw, Panther's Run and the soon-to-open Tiger's Eye located at Ocean Ridge Plantation in Sunset Beach, N.C.

Throughout his career, Plankers has worked at some of the finest golf courses in the country. At the age of 12, he was a caddy at Richland Golf and Country Club in Richland, Wash. The following year, young Tom was named shop manager and held the position until 1965. In 1970, Plankers joined the staff at Pine Valley Country Club in Wilmington, N.C., as an assistant pro. He held the same position at Cape Fear Country Club in Wilmington, N.C., 1973–74.

Plankers has been head golf professional and/or golf director at Oak Island Golf and Beach Club in Caswell Beach, N.C., Bald Head Island Country Club in Bald Head Island, N.C., and Oak Island Golf & Country Club where he was also general manager.

Ocean Ridge Plantation • 351 Ocean Ridge Parkway S.W. • Sunset Beach NC 28469 • tel: 910.287.1717

OCEAN RIDGE
GOLF CLUB

LION'S PAW GOLF LINKS

PANTHER'S RUN GOLF LINKS

Lion's Paw Golf Links at Ocean Ridge Plantation in Sunset Beach, N. C., on the northern end of Myrtle Beach's Grand Strand, is an open, hilly course that treats the golfer to spectacular views of a beautiful creek valley and its adjoining wetlands. Lion's Paw is distinguished by towering hardwoods, boldly-contoured bent grass greens, spectacular water shots, and mounds of sugar white sand marking deep bunkers and high embankments. At Lion's Paw, oyster shells line the lakes around par three's and creeks flow across wide, rolling bermuda grass fairways.

The 18-hole Willard Byrd design features bent grass greens, more than 70 bunkers, and generous mounding lining many fairways. Water comes into play on 15 holes and beautiful wetland views can be seen from several holes. The first 12 holes of the course feature tree-lined fairways and lots of doglegs creating a true "shot maker's" golf course. Staring with hole 13, the fairways run through wide open spaces where the wind definitely becomes a factor.

Lion's Paw measures 7,003 yards from the blue tees; 6,457 yards from the white tees; 5,872 yards from the gold tees; and 5,363 yards from the red tees, and is a par 72. Tee Times can be arranged by calling 1-800-233-1801 or accessing the Ocean Ridge Plantation website at http://www.oceanridge.com/golf.

Panther's Run at Ocean Ridge Plantation in Sunset Beach, N. C. on the northern end of Myrtle Beach's Grand Strand, is designed to test the golfer's skill, but not break his game.

Designer Tim Cate followed the natural terrain of the North Carolina coast in crafting this course which is visually captivating as well as challenging. The 18-hole layout meanders through rolling, wooded land with rambling brooks, and huge ponds. Cate has provided generous landing areas in the bermuda grass fairways and large bent grass greens. He has incorporated many environmentally sensitive areas into the overall the course, adding to its stunning beauty. On many holes, the cart paths border a spectacular and pristine nature preserve that is home to a wide variety of wildlife.

Panther's Run measures 7,089 yards from the back tees; 6,706 yards from the blue tees; 6,267 yards from the white tees; and two forward tees measure 5,546 yards and 5,023 yards.

Tee Times can be arranged by calling 1-800-233-1801 or accessing the Ocean Ridge Plantation website at http://www.oceanridge.com/golf.

The Ocean Ridge Plantation Golf Shoppe, which serves both Lion's Paw and Panther's Run, is one of America's Top 100 Golf Shops (GSO Magazine 1997, 1998, 1999).

ACKNOWLEDGMENTS

TIM

Tim Jackson is the head golf professional at the Legends Resorts in Myrtle Beach, S.C. In 1986, he graduated with a business administration degree from Coastal Carolina University where he also played competitive golf. Jackson has been at the Legends since 1992 and is responsible for devising lesson plans for the golf staff and conducting lessons, clinics and golf schools.

Jackson also oversees all aspects of daily operations for Legends Resorts' three on-site courses — Heathland, Parkland and Moorland. He is responsible for the professional staff, starters, rangers and cart attendants as well as budgeting, purchasing, merchandising and controlling inventory with annual sales exceeding $1,000,000. Jackson also oversees Legends Resorts summer tournament schedule including the South Carolina State Amateur and the DuPont World Amateur.

Before coming to the Legends Resorts, Jackson was an assistant golf professional at Marsh Harbour Golf Links, one of Legends Resorts five off-site courses.

Legends • PO Box 2038 • Myrtle Beach, SC 28578 • tel: 800.530.1872 • www.legendsgolf.com • e-mail: legends@sccoast.net

MOORLAND AT LEGENDS

Legends Resorts in the center of the Grand Strand is a 1,300-acre, upscale Scottish-inspired golf resort located 10 minutes from the Atlantic Ocean and the Myrtle Beach International Airport.

Legend's 42,000-square-foot clubhouse, which can be seen from many holes on the resort's three on-site courses, is reminiscent of the Royal & Ancient Golf Club in St. Andrews, Scotland. Adjacent to the clubhouse is one of America's Top 100 practice facilities (Golf Range Report); villa accommodations in a charming Scottish village complete with pub, pools, and lighted putting greens; and a residential community where clusters of homes are arranged around their own private mini-parks.

The award-winning Moorland course was named one of the Top 5 New Courses In America when it opened (*Golf Digest* magazine). Designed by P. B. Dye, the par 72 layout is reminiscent of the PGA West Stadium Course.

Known for its sculpted terrain and elevation changes, Moorland is considered one of the strongest golf challenges on the East Coast. A true "target" golf course, it requires golfers to maneuver around vast expanses of sand, large waste areas, cavernous bunkers, and huge lakes. Moorland has bermuda fairways, bermuda rough, and bent grass greens.

The course measures 6,799 yards from the tournament gold tees; 6,143 yards from the green tees; and 4,905 yards from the red tees. The course is rated and sloped at 73.1/128 from the tournament gold tees; 69.8/121 from the green tees; and 71.0/127 from the red tees. Information about Legends golf and golf packages, as well as real estate, is available by calling 800-530-1872, or on the Internet at http://www.legendsgolf.com.

In addition to Moorland, Legends offers its guests five other courses—Heathland and Parkland on site at Legends and Oyster Bay, Marsh Harbour and Heritage a short driving distance away.

PETE

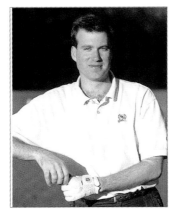

Peter Hymes is the head golf professional at the Heritage Golf Club on Pawleys Island, S.C. In 1992, Hymes graduated from Principia College (Elsah, Ill.) with a degree in business administration and French. He has been the head pro at the Heritage Golf Club since 1996.

Hymes, a Class-A PGA professional, conducts annual golf clinics and gives individual lessons that stress simplicity in the golf swing. In addition to teaching, Hymes is responsible for the entire golf operations at the Heritage Clubís 18-hole facility.

Hymes has been with The Legends Group a management company based in Myrtle Beach, S.C., that operates six area courses (Heritage Club, Oyster Bay, Marsh Harbour, Heathland, Parkland and Moorland) and two in Williamsburg, Va., (Royal New Kent and Legends of Stonehouse) since 1992. Hymes has served as the head golf professional at Heathland and as an assistant pro at Heritage Golf Club and Oyster Bay Golf Links.

Heritage Club

HERITAGE CLUB

Heritage Club is the centerpiece of beautiful Heritage Plantation, built on the site of the historic rice plantations, True Blue and Midway, near Pawleys Island, S.C., on the southern end of the Grand Strand. Part of the Legends Resorts family of golf courses, Heritage Club opened in 1986, and is ranked among the top 50 public courses in America (*Golf Digest* magazine).

Heritage Club has a spectacular Lowcountry setting. A magnificent avenue of centuries-old oaks leads to the 12,000-square-foot antebellum-style clubhouse and heavily landscaped areas of wildflowers and flowering shrubs add to the enchanting natural beauty of this challenging golf course.

Flanked by giant magnolias and 300-year-old oaks, Heritage Club features spacious, rolling bermuda fairways and large, undulating bent grass greens, surrounded by lush stands of crepe myrtle, camellias and azaleas. Numerous fresh water lakes, the remains of ancient ricefields and riverside marsh come into play throughout the course.

The par 71 course measures 7,040 yards from the tournament gold tees; 6,565 yards from the blue tees; 6,090 yards from the white tees; and 5,325 yards from the red tees. The course is rated and sloped at 74.1/137 from the tournament gold tees; 72.0/128 from the blue tees; 69.6/117 from the white tees; and 71.0/125 from the red tees.

Information about tee times at Heritage Club or Legends golf packages is available by calling 800-530-1872, or on the Internet at http://www.legendsgolf.com.

ACKNOWLEDGMENTS

MEL

Mel Sole played on the Pro Tour in his native South Africa from 1970 to 1980. During this period he discovered his love and talent for teaching golf. Two of his junior teams became national champions. Several of his individual golfers earned national recognition as well.

In 1984 Sole opened the Canadian Golf Academy in Toronto. In 1988, his long-time friend and mentor Phil Ritson hired Sole to head the Phil Ritson Golf School in Myrtle Beach, S.C. The school relocated to Pawleys Plantation Golf & County Club in Pawleys Island, S.C. Today the Phil Ritson-Mel Sole Golf School is recognized as one of the best in America. Increasing demand for its instruction services has prompted the expansion of operations to five sites across the southern and eastern United States.

Sole is also a teaching editor with *Golf Tips* magazine and *On the Green* magazine.

Phil Ritson-Mel Sole Golf School• 70 Tanglewood Drive • Pawleys Island, SC 29585 • tel: 843.237.4993l

PAWLEYS PLANTATION
GOLF & COUNTRY CLUB

PAWLEYS PLANTATION

The Jack Nicklaus signature golf course at Pawleys Plantation in Pawleys Island, S. C. is the heart of a very special 582-acre golfing retreat at the southern end of the Grand Strand. In addition to its spectacular par 72 layout that winds through hardwood and pine forests, and along the saltwater marsh dividing Pawleys Island from the mainland, Pawleys Plantation is home to the Phil Ritson-Mel Sole School of Golf, one of the Top 25 Golf Schools In America (*Golf Magazine*).

The Plantation's award-winning course is a traditional layout that Nicklaus calls "one of my best." He designed the course "to capture the natural terrain and complement and enhance the beauty of the salt marsh and Low country."

Landing areas in the bermuda grass fairways are generous, and the bent grass greens are large, but the course does require golfers to think their way around the 18 holes—in keeping with Nicklaus' belief that golf "is game of precision as well as power."

The front nine of Pawleys Plantation features tree-lined fairways and beautiful lakes, while the back nine delivers spectacular views of the salt marsh from six different holes. The signature hole, the par 3 number 13, is bulkheaded into the marsh and offers breathtaking views and exceptional challenges.

From the back or "Golden Bear" tees, Pawleys Plantation measures 7,026 yards with a slope of 140 and a 74.8 rating. Other yardages, slopes and ratings are as follows: Blue Heron tees 6,522/133/71.9; White Egret tees 6,127/125/70.5; Red Tail Hawk tees 5,572/130/73; Yellow Finch tees 4,979/126/70.1. Golf is available to guests staying at Pawleys PlantationÕs secluded on-site villas.

Information is available by calling 800-367-9959, extension 6009, or on the Internet at http://www.pawleysplantation.com. The Ritson-Sole School, which provides instruction for individuals as well as programs for corporations and other groups, can be reached at phone 1- 800-624-4653 and http://www.ritson-sole.com.

ACKNOWLEDGMENTS

JENNY

A positive attitude and real talent as a player and teacher have made **Jennifer Buchanan** a star at the Phil Ritson-Mel Sole Golf School at Pawleys Plantation in Pawleys Island, S.C. Her impressive amateur career began as a member of the Wisconsin state-champion high school golf team in 1984. She was Wisconsin State Amateur Stroke Play Champion in 1987 and Match Play runner-up in the same year. Buchanan co-captained the golf team at the University of Miami (Fla.) and was a five-time U.S. Amateur Qualifier and twice the medallist. She turned professional in 1989 and competed on the Futures Tour from 1989 to 1992. She also played on the Ladies Asian Tour in 1991 and 1992.

Jenny's eight-year teaching career includes tutelage under Bob Toski, David Leadbetter, Davis Love II and Bob Rotella. She joined the Phil Ritson-Mel Sole Golf School in 1996.

Pawleys Plantation Golf & Country Club• 70 Tanglewood Drive • Pawleys Island, SC 29585 • tel: 843.237.6100

Pawleys Plantation
GOLF & COUNTRY CLUB

JASON

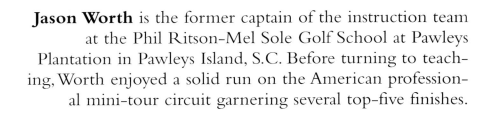

Jason Worth is the former captain of the instruction team at the Phil Ritson-Mel Sole Golf School at Pawleys Plantation in Pawleys Island, S.C. Before turning to teaching, Worth enjoyed a solid run on the American professional mini-tour circuit garnering several top-five finishes.

Worth played for four years on the Texas Christian University golf team. After his mini-tour career, he brought his extensive competitive experience and strong background in sports psychology to the Ritson-Sole Golf School in 1996. Worth trained under Mel Sole and has since become an outstanding teacher to golfers of all ages and abilities.

ACKNOWLEDGMENTS

RICK

PGA Class-A professional **Richard Shoemaker** recently became the director of golf at The International World Tour Golf Links near Myrtle Beach, S.C. This 27-hole facility re-creates more than two dozen of the world's greatest golf holes. As a contributor to this book, Shoemaker was head golf professional at Tidewater Golf Club & Plantation. The Tidewater Golf Club is an enchanting course set on a forested peninsula that overlooks the Intracoastal Waterway and Atlantic Ocean in North Myrtle Beach.

Prior to joining Tidewater, Shoemaker was head golf professional at Cypress Bay Golf Club near Myrtle Beach. At the same time, he manned the helm at nearby Colonial Charters Golf Club. Shoemaker also has worked for the Man of War Teaching Center, a state-of-the-art golf teaching center in Lexington, Ky., where he specialized in its acclaimed juniors' teaching program. Shoemaker is a graduate of James Madison University.

Tidewater Golf Club & Plantation • 4901 Little River Neck Road • North Myrtle Beach, SC 29582 • tel: 800.446.5363

TIDEWATER
GOLF CLUB & PLANTATION

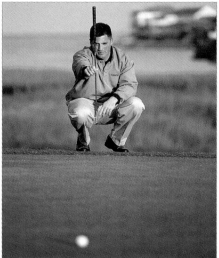

TIDEWATER GOLF CLUB

Tidewater Golf Club and Plantation, situated on a magnificent seaside peninsula in North Myrtle Beach, S. C., is one of the premier residential communities in the United States. It award-winning championship 18-hole golf course is the most honored course on the Grand Strand and it remains the only golf course ever named Best New Public Course in America by both *Golf Digest* and *Golf Magazine* in the same year. From 1990 to present, Tidewater has consistently been ranked the No. 1 course in Myrtle Beach, S.C. (*Golf Digest*).

A classic design, Tidewater is modeled after renowned courses such as such as Merion and Pine Valley. Its bermuda grass fairways and bent grass greens flow with the natural contours of the land. Numerous elevation changes, unusual for the Grand Strand area, add to the beauty and uniqueness of the course.

Many of Tidewater's holes play alongside the Intracoastal Waterway and saltwater marshes of Cherry Grove Beach Inlet and several offer breathtaking views of the Atlantic Ocean. Its location allows golfers to observe a variety of wildlife and, from the ocean side of the course, golfers can even see dolphins swimming in the inlet.

The heart of its thriving residential community, Tidewater measures 7,150 yards from the black tees; 6,530 yards from the blue tees; 6,000 yards from the white tees; 5,090 yards from the gold tees; and 4,665 yards from the green tees. A public course, it is managed by Troon Golf, which is known worldwide for its commitment to excellence in course conditioning and customer service.

Information about Tidewater is available by calling 1–800–TIDE-234 or accessing the Tidewater Golf Club and Plantation website at http://www.tide-water.com.

Special Thanks

PRC Publishing would like to extend its gratitude to Lesnik, Himmelsbach, Wilson, Hearl & Hirsch Advertising & Public Relations (LHWH) of Myrtle Beach, S.C. Known as the "golf smart" agency, LHWH was instrumental in coordinating the logistics of our photographic adventure in and around Myrtle Beach. The pictures would never have come out as beautifully as they did without their help.

Over the years, LHWH has helped launch new product lines such as MAXFLI's Jan line of golf equipment and accessories, which pioneered the boutique concept for golf shops; Lady Fairway's entry into the golf shoe market; and SP Golf's introduction of the Bald Eagle golf balls. In addition, LHWH has publicized products for numerous other national equipment clients such as STX, Lange Golf, Square Two Golf, G-Loomis, Fenwick and Wood Bros Golf. LHWH has also been instrumental in raising the profile of numerous North and South Carolina golf course developments including Legends Resorts, Pawleys Plantation, Tidewater Golf Club and Plantation, and Ocean Ridge Plantation. Along the way, the avid golfers of the PR team have staged press conferences for some of the biggest names in golf, including Greg Norman, John Daly, Bob Murphy and Jan Stephenson.

When not focused on golf clients, LHWH's PR team has developed and implemented public relations strategies for a wide variety of travel and tourism clients. Among those are the national sales division of Hard Rock Café, the first Ripley's Aquarium, NASCAR SpeedPark and NASCAR Café and South Carolina's top shopping destination, the $250 million Broadway At The Beach entertainment complex.

LESNIK HIMMELSBACH WILSON HEARL & HIRSCH
Advertising and Public Relations

The people that make it happen are:
Lei Gainer, Director of Public Relations
Amanda Nelson, Public Relations Coordinator
Bridgette Moore Johnson, Public Relations Associate
Chris McCalmont, Public Relations Associate
Heather Phillips, Public Relations Assistant